During the year that Elvis has already been gone there have been many people promoting various Elvis products. How do you feel about that? Does that cheapen his memory or perpetuate it?

I feel that if they advertise products about Elvis — his real picture or likenesses of him — I don't think that cheapens his memory at all for that stuff to be publicized. Elvis' records released on RCA — I don't believe that that hurts his image in any way because it actually shows him as he was. But for people to imitate him, that's the thing that defames his memory. I sat there in a hotel in Las Vegas watching somebody do Elvis, and I watched the reaction of the people. It was kind of like, "Man, that's really the way he was. It's too bad, you know." The guy happened to look a lot like Elvis and he sang like he would expect Elvis to sing if he had just had a hand grenade go off in his back and he could barely move, and he was ready to fall into his grave. That's how he would expect Elvis to sound. When Elvis sang his last concert he sounded like he was at his peak.

OTHER BOOKS
BY
THE SAME AUTHOR

PAUL MC CARTNEY—
BEATLE WITH WINGS

THE KING IS DEAD:
ELVIS PRESLEY

BEATLE MADNESS

# ELVIS — THE LEGEND LIVES!

## Martin A. Grove

MANOR
BOOKS
INC.

*DEDICATION*

*For Marjorie Joan & Geoffrey Eric.*

**A MANOR BOOK**

Manor Books, Inc.
432 Park Avenue South
New York, New York 10016

ISBN CODE 0-532-19196-X

# ELVIS—THE LEGEND LIVES!

## Table Of Contents

# CHAPTER ONE

## ELVIS — THE LEGEND LIVES!

*"To live in hearts we leave
behind is not to die," Thomas
Campbell once wrote.*

More than a year has passed since August 16, 1977, the day Elvis died. And, at times, it is difficult if not impossible to believe that the months have flown by so quickly.

There is something about the death of a public figure such as Elvis that makes people remember where they were when they first learned of his passing. I recall, for instance, that when the news bulletins broke about JFK's assassination I was having lunch at the Playboy Club in New York City.

I first heard that Elvis had died while I was whizzing along a freeway in Los Angeles.

While the circumstances were very difficult in the two deaths there was in both cases the same need to talk to other people about what had happened. There was the same wishful thinking that one had heard the bulletin wrong, or that the announcer had made a mistake, or that the wire service had gotten its wires crossed.

And then, in both of these instances as well as many others, there was the ultimate realization that there hadn't been any mistake; that it was all too true.

Thomas Campbell, the English poet and editor, once wrote that, "To live in hearts we leave behind is not to die." I think that those are especially well chosen words with which to describe Elvis' death, although they were written well more than a century before the King of Rock 'n Roll came to power.

For in the months following Elvis' death we have come to realize that while Elvis may no longer be alive, he is far from forgotten. Indeed, there may be some truth to the suggestion that in death Elvis stands even taller than he did in his final years. While some people would argue that towards the end of his life Elvis was losing his grip on superstardom, letting go of himself physically, giving too much free reign to his emotions and seeing younger men assume the leadership he had commanded for so long in the music business, there seems little doubt but that in death Elvis has recaptured the spotlight that once was his.

I think it is entirely fair to say that Elvis, the legend, lives.

In Los Angeles, for example, from 11:00 p.m. until Midnight every night one radio station plays nothing but Elvis' records. The station promises its teenage listeners that it will never forget the King of Rock 'n Roll. Stations throughout the country are doing similar types of Elvis promotions. In some instances Elvis' hits have been added to radio stations' *solid gold* libraries, so that when it's time to have the disc jockey play an *oldie* he has the opportunity to reach for *Hound Dog* or *Love Me Tender* or *Are You Lonesome Tonight?* or some other classic Elvis song.

One radio syndication company updated its rock 'n roll history documentary, putting added emphasis on Elvis' contributions to the evolution of today's music. Another syndicator took its Elvis special program off the market until it could be brought up-to-date with the news of his death. When it was available for sale again radio stations everywhere were waiting to snap it up.

Television, too, has made certain that none of us has the opportunity to forget that Elvis filmed many quite forgettable movies. (In case you have forgotten, a complete filmography of Elvis' work on celluloid is included in this book.) From time to time some of Elvis' thirty-three movies pop up on the *Late Show, Early Show, Late Late Show,* or you-name-it. And just as they did terrific box office business when they were first released to theatres, they now draw impressive ratings when they are seen on TV.

There are more people impersonating Elvis in theatres or night clubs throughout the country these days than one might believe existed! They, too, help to perpetuate the memory of the legendary King of Rock 'n Roll. I had the opportunity to interview Alan Meyer, whose impressive tribute to Elvis has been seen by widespread audiences over the last five years. His fascinating thoughts about Elvis and his indictment of the Elvis imitators are contained in the following chapter.

On newsstands and in bookstores, too, it's impossible not to be reminded that Elvis has passed through this world of ours. Immediately after his death a number of magazine publishers rushed out special periodicals devoted to the life and career of Elvis. Every picture that was ever snapped of Elvis, or so it seemed, wound up in somebody's magazine.

Hundreds of thousands of Elvis magazines were sold throughout the world. In some cases publishers were fortunate in being able to get their versions of Elvis' story printed, distributed and put on sale before the strong public appetite for material about him was satiated. Luck played its part in this sometimes. One publisher was said to have been preparing a one-shot magazine about Elvis before he died, only to speed things up in the production department on hearing the news bulletins.

In another case, a paperback edition of a best-selling book about Elvis was scheduled for August release prior to Elvis' death. It probably would have sold very well under any circumstances, but coming out on the heels of his death it quickly became a giant.

Most leading newspapers across the U.S. devoted substantial front page space to reporting the details of Elvis' death. A great many of these papers ran large amounts of feature material about him inside their editions. Sometimes these features were compiled as special supplements or feature sections.

In short, there was no shortage of reportage about Elvis' last days. New books such as my own tribute to Elvis were written in the days following his passing. And old books were dug up by publishers who had long since forgotten they had once put them out. These were dusted off and reprinted, sometimes with a bonus paragraph or mini-chapter concerning Elvis' death.

While some businesses probably took advantage of Elvis' passing to sell products about him to his saddened fans, there were various publishers and authors, myself among them, who were touched by his death and sought to pay him tribute in the most suitable and lasting way—by writing about him.

Although no tribute to Elvis can ever bring him back, the effect of all of these activities has been to keep his memory very much alive. Unlike so many of the early pioneers of the music form we call *rock* today, Elvis is not forgotten. Whereas people are sometimes heard to remark "Oh, I didn't know he was still alive" when they discover some one-time big rock 'n roll name playing some Las Vegas hotel lounge, they hear so much of Elvis nowadays that they could be forgiven for forgetting that he is no longer with us.

Of course, the one thing that we haven't as yet seen done to Elvis is the giant multi-million dollar Hollywood movie treatment of his life. There have been reports that various top producers planned to give Elvis the so-called *biopic* tribute, but nothing definite has been announced as these words are written.

This is, without any question, the era of the rock music movie. In recent times we have seen pioneer disc jockey Alan Freed, who is generally credited with having coined the phrase *rock 'n roll,* honored with a movie about his life *(American Hot Wax),* and we have seen a movie devoted to life's ups and downs at a supposedly typical American radio station *(FM).* Buddy Holly has been immortalized, as if that were necessary in view of the great work he left behind, in *The Buddy Holly Story.* The Bee Gees' music was a key selling point involved in the staggering success of *Saturday Night Fever* starring John Travolta. Then The Bee Gees went on to star with Peter Frampton in *Sgt. Pepper's Lonely Hearts Club Band,* an all-singing picture based on The Beatles' 1967 album of the same name.

With such Hollywood fascination with the music industry and its people it should follow readily that someday someone will work out the right deal to do *The Elvis Presley Story* on film. Like other pictures where the audience knows what's going to happen before they even buy their tickets, the success of such a film would depend on the ability of its actors to make the audience believe that the people on-screen were not actors but the real Elvis, Colonel Parker, etc.

If such a movie about Elvis' life were being cast today the first name that would come to mind to play Elvis would be John Travolta, who rose to the top of his acting profession with *Saturday Night Fever* and then went on to do the musical giant *Grease.*

I am somewhat surprised that as of this writing no one has produced a television movie based on Elvis' life and loosely translated to some fictional character. There's no doubt about it, a strong TV drama could be constructed around the story of a young singer from the South who helps pioneer a new form of pop music, rises to super-stardom—from being dirt poor to filthy rich!—and surrounds himself with paid bodyguards, gofers, buddies and beauties before he winds up being burnt out and destroyed by his success.

Once the word leaked out that this was really a film about Elvis, there's no question but that there would be an enormous audience for it. Probably the only reason that no one has mounted such a quickie production as yet is that Elvis' estate might have grounds for a lawsuit.

The concept of Elvis' estate still managing Elvis as an entertainment act may be difficult for some of his fans to comprehend. After all, how do you manage a dead man? Well, in Elvis' case, despite the fact that he is no longer here to make personal appearances, there are so many business opportunities for him nowadays that his long-time manager, Colonel Tom Parker, still has a full-time job!

In my interview with Alan Meyer for this book he puts it very well when he notes that Colonel Parker is, in effect, now managing Elvis' memory. Acting for Elvis' father, Vernon Presley, and Elvis' estate, the Colonel has supervised the development of a number of important merchandising activities involving Elvis.

The concept of merchandising a personality is relatively new to show business. One of the best examples of merchandising is the giant-sized poster. Millions of posters of people like Farrah Fawcett—

Majors, Suzanne Somers, John Travolta and Henry Winkler, for instance, have already been sold—for anywhere from $2 to $5 apiece! That addes up to a lot of money.

Of course, posters are just the most obvious type of merchandising tie-in. There are all sorts of other things that can be worked out to make money for a hot property. The *Star Wars* merchandising campaign, which will probably pass the $100 million mark by the end of 1978, is an excellent case in point.

Among the merchandising tie-ins already licensed by *Star Wars* and Twentieth Century-Fox are: posters, metal lunchboxes, R2D2 cookie jars, ceramic tankards, stormtrooper head masks, sleeping bags, paperback novels, proton torpedos, bubble gum cards, Darth Vadar costumes, pajamas, socks, comic books, photo albums, poster magazines, children's shoes, T-shirts, 8mm sound films of movie excerpts, X-wing fighter toys, microelectronic digital watches, children's wristwatches, leather belts with *Star Wars* buckles, notebooks, souvenir programs, necklaces featuring R2D2, Darth Vadar and C3PO, jewelry charms of R2D2 and C3PO, and metal plates of the *Star Wars* logo!

Before Elvis' death he and Colonel Parker established a company called Boxcar, Inc. to handle the exclusive marketing and licensing for "all commerical Elvis Presley rights." Soon after Elvis passed away Boxcar, Inc. made an agreement with the well-known merchandising firm Factors Etc., Inc. In return for granting its exclusive Elvis merchandising rights to Factors, Boxcar received a payment of $1000,000 against a guarantee of

$150,000, according to published reports. Of course, sales could bring in quite a bit more than $150,000.

But if there was going to be any value in having the merchandising rights to Elvis Presley, Factors would have to try to put a stop to any unlicensed merchandising activities involving the King of Rock 'n Roll.

Shortly after making its deal with Boxcar, Factors went to federal court in New York to stop the sale of Elvis posters and souvenirs by a card company there. The defendants argued, according to newspaper accounts, that Elvis' promotional rights did not survive him. Therefore, the defendants felt they had been free to produce and sell Elvis posters.

Judge Charles H. Tenney, who heard the case, decided otherwise. The court's action for the plaintiff (Factors Etc., Inc.) was made public in late October 1977, but the full court opinion was not published until the following February. In it Judge Tenney noted, "The 'right of publicity' is not a new concept, but to the detriment of legal clarity, it has often been discussed only under the rubric 'right of privacy'." He also stated that, "It is evident that courts address intrusions on feelings, reputation and privacy only when an individual has elected not to engage in personal commercialization.

"By contrast, when a 'persona' is in effect a product, and that product has already been marketed to good advantage, the appropriation by another of that valuable competition has more to do with unfair competition than it does with the right to be left alone.

"There is no reason why the valuable rights of

publicity—clearly exercised by and financially benefitting Elvis Presly in life—should not descend at death like any other intangible property right."

In setting its successful suit against the New York card company, Factors reported receiving over $250,000. As a part of the settlement, the card company was granted an official license to sell its Elvis posters, with a royalty for each one sold going to the license holder (Factors).

In another case, Factors was named as the defendant in a suit brought by a nonprofit organization that was raising money to erect a statue of Elvis in Memphis. As a fund-raising tactic, the group wanted to give anyone contributing at least $25 a pewter replica of the Elvis statue. The lawsuit against Factors was brought to keep the merchandising firm from interfering with the fund-raising giveaways of Elvis statues.

Factors was the victor in this case, too. Memphis District Judge Harry Wellford's opinion was that, "The well-reasoned cases, it is believed, set out a clear distinction between the valuable right of publicity or public figures such as Presley and the right of privacy in the sense of being left alone, free from harrassment or humiliation, in a torious claim.

"Elvis Presley himself, through Parker and Boxcar, fully pursued this exclusive right of publicity during his lifetime. The party holding this exclusive right during lifetime and the personal representative of Elvis Presley, after his death, unequivocally attempted to assign (Factors) exclusive rights to the name and image as it related to the kind of statuary involved in this proceeding."

In the past the right of privacy and the right of

publicity had been tied together. Previous cases involving the heirs of Jesse James and Al Capone had been lost because the courts decided that there was no *invasion of privacy* by movies based on the lives of James or Capone since those rights ceased to exist when the people, themselves died.

Subsequently, the heirs of comedians Stan Laurel and Oliver Hardy brought a suit against Hal Roach Studios, claiming that the rights to Laurel and Hardy's likenesses were theirs and not the studio's. The decision in that case was that Laurel and Hardy's creation of a property right survived their deaths.

Finally, there had been a similar case brought to court in California some years after the Laurel and Hardy decision in New York. The heirs of Bela Lugosi, who was famous as the movie actor who portrayed Count Dracula, took Universal Pictures to court, arguing that they and not Universal owned the rights to Lugosi's likeness. But in this case the court's decision was that Universal could proceed because Bela Lugosi had never made it a point to exploit his Dracula character himself.

The suits brought to court involving Elvis were unique, however, in that they happened almost immediately after his death. Previous cases in which various heirs had turned to the courts for relief didn't take place until the personalities involved had been dead for years.

As a result of the guidelines established by the New York and Memphis federal judges in the two Presley related suits, performers should be able to take steps in the future to guarantee that their names and likenesses are not appropriated by others for commercial exploitation after their deaths.

Elvis' estate had more to worry about than just the taking of his likeness, though. Not long after his death a plot was uncovered in which three men were accused of trying to steal Elvis' body! The story first hit the newspapers on August 30, 1977. It was reported that three men have been foiled by a Memphis police stakeout in their possible efforts to remove Elvis' body from his mausoleum and hold it for ransom.

But the police found no hard evidence to support such a charge, and only cited them for trespassing. In Tennessee trespassing is a misdeameanor, and the trio was released on bond.

According to the papers, the three Memphis men—Raymond M. Green, 25, Bruce Eugene Nelson, 30, and Ronnie Lee Adkins, 26—were arrested after a car chase by the police, who had seen them creeping up to the front door of Elvis' mausoleum. No burglary tools were found in their possession, although the police said they thought the tools had been thrown out of the men's car during the chase.

The day after this story broke another newspaper account appeared in which it was reported that one of the three men, Ronnie Lee Adkins, had been identified as having tipped the police to the plot to snatch Elvis' body for ransom.

It was not until October 5 that the case was closed with the announcement that charges against the trio had been dropped. Prosecutor Robert Donahue was quoted as having told Memphis City Court Judge John Dwyer, "We can't stand behind any statement made by him [Ronnie Lee Adkins]. His statements were so unreliable that we cannot vouch for his information.

The city's Police Director E. Winslow Chapman acknowledged that the body-snatching story may, indeed, have been a hoax. But he did say, according to reports, that Mr. Adkins had previously given reliable information to the police in other cases.

An attorney representing Mr. Green and Mr. Nelson was quoted as explaining, "They [his clients] were not there to steal the body. He [ Mr. Adkins] had lured them out there under some false pretenses." Calling Mr. Adkins "a man of persuasion," attorney Jay Fred Friedman went on to charge, "He just thought he could get a big story to sell. It wasn't exactly a money deal and it wasn't anything about stealing a body."

A wire service report at the time attributed to Mr. Adkins the story that an unidentified man had promised to pay the trio $40,000 to make-off with Elvis' body. That man, in turn, had intended to hold the corpse until he received $10 million in ransom for it.

the bodies of both Elvis and his mother, which had been buried within the same mausoleum, were then removed on Sunday night, October 2, 1977 from Forest Hill Cemetery and re-buried in the "meditation gardens" on the 13-acre Graceland estate. On November 27, 1977 the gates of Graceland Mansion were thrown open to the public for the very first time.

From Tuesdays through Sundays Graceland was opened by Vernon Presley so that Elvis' fans could pay tribute to him in person from late morning to early afternoon. "I still have a little work to do to get them [the graves] perfect, but we just couldn't hold back the people any longer," Mr. Presley was quoted as having explained.

Shortly before this decision to open Graceland to the public, Vernon Presley made some news of his own. On November 15 it was reported that his second wife, Davada, had obtained a Dominican Republic divorce from him, after seventeen years of marriage. They had been married two years after Elvis' mother, Gladys, had died.

One of the controversies that sprang up following Elvis' passing was whether drugs played a part in his sudden death. There were those who thought that they did, although they had absolutely no evidence upon which to base the gossip they spread. On October 22, 1977 newspaper reports revealed that in the opinion of Dr. Jerry T. Francisco, the medical examiner, forShelby County, Memphis, Elvis' death was caused by hypertensive heart disease, not drugs.

But Dr. Francisco did report that postmortem tests on Elvis' body had discovered significant amounts of four drugs as well as amounts of four other drugs that would not have had any pharmacological effect on his body.

"Had these drugs not been there, he still would have died," Dr. Francisco was quoted as saying. The four drugs found in Elvis' body, he explained, were not found in quantities larger than what would constitute normal therapeutic levels. The drugs included ethinamate and methaquaalone, two sedatives; codiene, which Elvis was taking on prescription due to some dental work he had done; and barbiturates.

Two days later there were newspaper reports that officials at Baptist Hospital in Memphis did not believe that Elvis died only from heart disease. It was reported that a confidential hospital autopsy report called Elvis' death "polypharmacy" (drug-related).

In all likelihood those who want to believe that drugs played a part in Elvis' death will always think so, and those who choose to believe that his death was not related to drugs will always hold to that view. Beyond the autopsy already performed, there is nothing that can be done to provide an answer.

Although there may be argument over precisely what resulted in Elvis' death, there is no question as to what he left behind. Some of the details regarding Elvis' estate were reported in newspapers of November 24, 1977. For instance, Elvis had five accounts in a Memphis bank, including one checking account which contained $1,055,173 at his death. This account, like all ordinary checking accounts, was not drawing any interest!

Vernon Presley filed an eighty-two page report in Memphis court, listing item-by-item what Elvis had left behind at Graceland Mansion. There were, for example, one hundred pairs of pants, many guns, sixteen TV sets (two of which were built directly into the ceiling over the nine by nine foot bed in which Elvis slept), eight automobiles, six motorcycles, two airplanes, lots of jewelry of all sorts, four horses, one colt and one pony.

Not included in this list were things like Elvis' royalties, his real estate holdings and various contract rights he held. Speculation was that these would be worth many millions more. To this day no full accounting of these has, to the best of my knowledge, found its way into the public press.

Elvis' grandmother, his father and his daughter, Lisa Marie, who was nine years old at the time, were named as the singer's beneficiaries.

On October 3, 1977 CBS-TV telecast a special film, *Elvis In Concert,* which had been shot the previous June during The King's Final concert tour. While Elvis performed the cameras were capturing his renditions of songs like *How Great Thou Art, Hurt* and *My Way.* The concerts that went into this production were done in Omaha, Nebraska and Rapid City, South Dakota.

At the time, Elvis was badly overweight and, as one newspaper reviewer put it, "only a fraction of his once-dynamic self. Considering his condition, it's surprising that he or manager Tom Parker agreed to allow the...concerts to be taped."

*Elvis in Concert* was produced by Gary Smith and Dwight Hemion, who are both respected television producers with a long list of credits, including Neil Diamond's television special from the Greek Theatre in Los Angeles. Their concept was to show Elvis on tour, and they held to that concept despite his death before the show was to air.

At the program's conclusion there was a brief appearance by Vernon Presley, surrounded by some of the piles of mail that had poured in expressing sorrow over Elvis' death. Mr. Presley thanked Elvis' fans for their messages of condolence, and as the camera turned away he appeared to be crying, something millions of television viewers throughout the country may also have been doing at that moment.

Later that same night in Los Angeles one of the local television stations offered Elvis in *Love Me Tender* on its late movie show. Most likely, TV stations in many cities honored Elvis with a showing of one of his pictures. And these probably represent a better way for fans to remember Elvis than the television documentary about his final concert tour. The Elvis from *Love Me Tender* and the Elvis from *Elvis In Concert* looked like two different people, and the first of them was considerably more attractive.

Some of the imitations of Elvis that were done throughout the period following his death in theatres or night clubs around the country were less than attractive, too. The skill of some Elvis imitators was better than others, and some were more honest than others in how they attempted to present The King.

An effort was made in February 1978 to curtail, if not entirely stop, the imitations. At that time Broadcast Music, Inc., one of the nation's two principal song licensing agencies—the other is ASCAP, the American Society of Composers, Authors and Publishers—informed performers and theatre owners that it was imposing strict new controls on the use of Elvis' songs.

Essentially, the new limitations imposed by BMI restrict its licensees "from permitting live public vocal performance at any one time of more than three musical compositions in order to protect the dramatic rights therein." This was stated in a letter sent by BMI to all of its licensees, reportedly at the request of various publishers wishing to protect their rights to songs associated with Elvis over the years.

For the most part, ordinary nightclub acts should not be affected by BMI's restrictions because most nightclub performers use a variety of material and should be able to avoid using more than three Elvis songs by any one publisher. But the acts that are severely affected by the BMI action are those that depend *entirely* on Elvis' songs.

"When you start weaving ten or twelve songs into a tribute or other obvious 'Presley' productions, you have to obtain special rights to the music," BMI Vice President Russell Sanjek was quoted as saying. Someone who wanted to obtain such special rights might very well find them to be quite costly.

BMI may have taken this step after witnessing the strong box office success of *Beatlemania,* the state tribute to The Beatles' music in which four young men dressed and made up in the style of The Beatles—but not calling themselves The Beatles—play an entire evening of music by John Lennon and Paul McCartney. The producers of *Beatlemania,* David Krebs and Steve Leber, obtained performance rights to the songs used in their production. If they hadn't, they would never have gotten away with opening *Beatlemania.* Needless to say, *Beatlemania* has been so successful that it has provided the music publishers involved with hefty royalties, already estimated to be worth several hundred thousand dollars.

Unlike Lennon and McCartney, Elvis didn't write most of his material. The Beatles' music was published by Northern Songs, which their manager, Brian Epstein, and their first music publisher, Dick James, had established in January 1963. It became a publicity held company two years later, by which time it had acquired the first fifty-nine Lennon and McCartney songs originally owned by the duo's Lenmac Enterprises. So it was comparatively easy to negotiate for the performance rights to The Beatles' music.

In Elvis' case, a number of music publishing firms held the rights to the songs he made famous. For instance, Sam Phillips, on whose Sun Records in Memphis Elvis' first records came out, has music publishing company called Hi Lo, which controls the rights to *Blue Suede Shoes* and *Mystery Train*. Mr. Phillips, reportedly, said he would not try to prevent any artist from performing either of those Elvis hits.

*Suspicious Minds* is owned by Screen Gems, *Heartbreak Hotel* by Tree and *Burning Love* by Combine, all music publishing firms. But most of the biggest Elvis hits are controlled by three publishers—Gladys, Elvis Presley Music and Hudson/Lieber & Stoller. These three firms have the rights to *Hound Dog, Don't Be Cruel, Love Me Tender, I Want You, I Need You, I Love You, Can't Help Falling In Love* and *Teddy Bear*. This is the group of songs that would probably be essential for any successful show about Elvis.

The effect of BMI's action was to make it difficult and costly to imitate Elvis Presley. Naturally, Elvis' imitators were not happy about this. There are, of course, a wide range of imitators. I am tempted to say that of all of them Alan Meyer may be the very best, but he does not consider that a compliment. In his words, "That just puts me at the top of the garbage heap."

I am willing to go along with Alan's view that what he is doing is *paying tribute* to Elvis, but BMI indicated otherwise. Prior to the opening in Los Angeles of Alan's show, *Elvis Forever,* he received a cable from the attorneys representing BMI. According to that wire, "Publicity about the show indicates it involves a dramatic production and an exercise of dramatic or grand performance rights in the music in it. Our clients intend to take appropriate steps to enforce their rights."

Alan's manager, Chet Actis, said that the show would go on—and indeed it did! "We regard BMI's suggestion as taking away Alan's right to sing Elvis," he was quoted as saying. "Alan is the originator of the tribute-to-Elvis concert and has been performing this for the last five years with no problems. He has even performed in Las Vegas at the same time as Presley."

Mr. Actis went on to point out that, in his opinion, Alan's show does not involve "dramatic rights" because Alan doesn't actually impersonate Elvis on stage. "He comes out as Alan, an Elvis fan, and does Elvis songs," he explained. "He doesn't say, 'I'm Elvis.' He says, 'I'm Alan.' "

At this writing, Alan's show has not been stopped by the BMI action. Other performers' use of Elvis' material has continued, as well. If efforts are made by BMI to enforce its limitations on using more than three songs from the same publisher, there will undoubtedly be actions and counter actions in the courts. It's possible that just as Elvis had had a major influence on shaping contemporary merchandising laws, he may also have an affect on the music publishing laws.

In the following chapter Alan Meyer goes into the situation involving performance rights to Elvis' music in greater detail, along with his own feelings about the late King of Rock 'n Roll.

The points noted in this chapter represent some of the most important developments in connection with Elvis throughout the first year following his death. They make it abundantly clear that Elvis' death was not the end of his career, but merely the end of new Elvis material and in-person appearances. Elvis' songs are with us today more than ever.

After Elvis' death there was a tremendous surge in purchases of his albums. Sales of various Elvis LPs continued to boom throughout the year. Record stores now stock and sell Elvis albums for which there had been less demand in the last years of his life.

Perhaps the true measure of Elvis' greatness is that it's exceedingly difficult to find anyone else in the history of pop music who equaled him. For example, if we say that Elvis was the dominant musical figure of the mid-1950s to mid-1960s, we can then say that The Beatles were the dominant musical figures of the mid-1960s to 1970. But The Beatles, of course, were four people, not one individual. And if we try to come up with an individual artist or even a group to equal Elvis and The Beatles in terms of 1970 to today, it's impossible to nominate anyone who will be readily acceptable to everyone.

To some people The Bee Gees are today's giant. But their dominance is really only of the moment. Time will tell if they have the same staying power that Elvis had. Fleetwood Mac might be another possible answer to the question, or maybe Elton

John. There's no question that they all sell a lot of records, but are they really today's equivalent to Elvis or The Beatles?

The line of descent from Elvis to The Beatles seems to end in our own time. Elvis is dead. The Beatles have split up and gone out on their own with varying degrees of success. And no one else has appeared to take their place—and keep it.

The legendary giants of contemporary music are gone. Only their legends live on after them.

# CHAPTER TWO

## ELVIS FOREVER — A TRIBUTE BY ALAN!

*"There's no greater tribute
to Elvis than himself. Nothing
can surpass him," Alan explained.*

Elvis Presley has been gone now for over a year. It's proof again of just how quickly time flies. During that period of time some 200 Elvis imitators' have sprung up throughout the world. It has been estimated that they have grossed some $3 million at the box office!

Twenty-seven year old Alan Meyer, a former electronics engineer with no previous show business background, has been doing a theatrical tribute to Elvis entitled *Elvis Forever* since before The King's death. Of all the imitators, Alan is the biggest in the field. It's said that he will gross a million dollars in 1978 alone.

With some justification Alan has gone on the record complaining about references to him as the "best Elvis Presley impersonator."

Alan's view has been that, "I do not consider it flattering to be considered the best imitator. That just puts me at the top of the garbage heap. As a matter of plain fact, I'm the worst Elvis imitator because I don't imitate him at all. I happen to sound like him—I can't control that. But I don't want to be categorized with the imitators. I like to think I pay tribute."

Alan has also pointed out that unlike most of the others now doing Elvis' material, "ninety per cent of what I do on stage was created before Elvis' death. I've been doing my show, more or less in the same form, long before he died. And I was successful with it. I broke records in Las Vegas and was the very first to take the Tribute to that city, sometimes even when Elvis, himself, was playing there. I took it to the Far East, to South Africa and to Israel. In fact, I was the only successful Elvis Tribute show working before his death."

An opportunity presented itself for me to talk to Alan Meyer—who is known professionally as, simply, Alan—while he was playing in Los Angeles at the Aquarius Theatre in June 1978. I found him to be a fascinating and articulate person with a strong love for Elvis. His candid views, which are presented in the following dialogue, represent Alan's opinions, but not necessarily those of the author or publisher, of course.

I began my interview with Alan by asking how he first became interested in Elvis Presley.

A:    I was about seven or eight years old. I heard *Teddy Bear* on the radio. Up until that time I never really was interested in music. I never thought much about it or listened to the radio or anything. I heard *Teddy Bear* coming from somewhere. I was walking out my front door and heard it, I guess, on a car radio. I just sat down on the lawn and listened to the whole song. It was like it put me in another world. I couldn't believe that any sound could have that affect on me. The smoothness in Elvis' voice. The way he rolled it so naturally. It was really just the greatest thing I had ever heard. I started listening from then on to everything he did. Every time he came out with a new song it was like a new treat. I couldn't wait to hear it when I heard he had a new song. When I got to be about twelve years old and I had an allowance I was able to buy records. When I went to the store to buy an Elvis record, I couldn't wait to get home to play it. I used to sing along with his records like a lot of kids did. When I first started doing it, I guess I was about eight. The only people who ever heard me were members of my family. My sister was an Elvis fan. She was about thirteen then. She was one of the originals. When Elvis came to Los Angeles she tried to sneak in the back exit to his dressing room— and didn't make it! She and all her friends at school were among the first Elvis fans.

MAG: How did she feel about your singing Elvis' songs?

A: Well, it freaked her out. She wanted me to sing it for her friends.

MAG: Because you had the right sound even then?

A: She said I sounded like an eight year old Elvis. As I grew up singing along with those records my voice started to get like his when I'd sing. Even if I sang a song by Paul Anka or Rick Nelson it still had more of an Elvis sound to it. By the time I was about fourteen or fifteen I think I was just about exactly the way he sounded at nineteen or twenty when he was doing *That's All Right, Mama*. I mean, there was no variation or difference. I couldn't tell the difference myself when I used to record it. But I still didn't sound like he did at what I consider to be the peak of the Elvis sound when he was about twenty-two—when he did *Treat Me Nice* and *Teddy Bear* and *Jailhouse Rock* and *Big Hunk Of Love* and *Don't* and *Loving You*. I just kept on singing along with his records just as a personal thing. Whenever I was asked to sing in front of a group I never would. The only people who ever heard me sing were close friends, girl friends, a good buddy, or my family. By the time I was twenty I sounded like him quite a bit. By the time I was about twenty-four I not only sounded like he did on *That's All Right, Mama*, but I sounded like he did on *The Wonder Of You*, which was in 1969. My voice had expanded so that I covered most everything he did identically. I would never be satisfied with anything less than that. It was about that time that I decided that I wanted to put a show together. I had never really thought about doing an Elvis show before. I never liked Elvis imitators. I thought that they deframed him. I thought that imitation was not the biggest form of flattery, but the biggest form of insult. To reproduce Elvis' voice in imitation inaccurately doesn't show the impact that his voice has on human beings. It's the sound of his voice that made him the King of Rock 'n Roll. It's the sound of his voice that knocked me over when I was eight years old. It wasn't because of his style. It wasn't because his voice hiccoughed and went down in tone. It was the way it sounded on every part on everything he sang.

MAG: So there were Elvis imitators even before his death.

A: There have been Elvis imitators since Elvis began. People used to get up and do one or two Elvis songs in 1957. In 1973 there used to be guys who would do a few songs by Johnny Cash and a few songs by some other country and western singer and a few songs by Tom Jones and they'd have to throw in Elvis. He was always thrown in.

MAG: But did they have shows that were entirely about Elvis?

A: No.

MAG: It's since his death, then, that we've seen

shows that revolve entirely around him.

A:     Except for my show.

MAG:   Had Elvis ever seen your show?

A:     He'd seen it on TV. He'd never seen it in its entirety. Not that I know of.

MAG:   How did he feel about the fact that you sang his material and sounded like he did?

A:     He really liked it. He really respected it, and he sent lots of good words to me. He said to somebody who talked to me that I know wouldn't lie because they worked for him, that as long as there was somebody like me around he knew that he'd be immortal. His voice and sound would never die. In 1973 I was twenty-four years old and I was really sick of other people who did imitations of Elvis, even though they did other people and even though it wasn't all about Elvis. They did at least two or three Elvis songs. And I figured that for people to take it that lightly they didn't really sound like him. But the people did clap and nod their heads like, "Yeah, that sounds like Elvis." And I remember commenting to a friend that if that guy sounded like Elvis the people wouldn't just sit there and go, "Yes, that sounds like Elvis," they'd be freaked out because that's what Elvis' voice does. Elvis' voice has a fat butterscotch sound. Anyway, I got together with some friends and sang some songs in front of them. It really did freak them out.

MAG:   When did you decide that you were going to do something professionally about Elvis?

A:    I sang in front of these friends and I had told them already how ridiculous I thought certain guys in town were who did a little bit of Elvis and didn't sound like him. They said they'd seen him, and thought the guy did sound like Elvis until they'd heard me! By hearing me they realized what I was talking about by others insulting him. They said their opinion of Elvis couldn't be that good if they thought that's what they sounded like. Hearing me made them realize that when you really do hear Elvis there's no two ways about it! They wanted me to show this to the world. They told me that there was this talent contest that very night in Silver Lake, which is in Washington. I was living there then and working for an electronics company. They encouraged me and pushed me and finally I went out there. I remember that when I finally did head up for the stage I heard a couple of comments that really scared me. I heard the words *Elvis* as I walked by! And I hadn't told anybody what I was going to sing. And I didn't want anybody to know because I didn't want them to prejudge me. I guess it's just the way I was dressed.

MAG:  The costume you wore suggested Elvis?

A:    I never wore a costume that suggested Elvis. It's just that anything I ever wore suggested Elvis! I wore black pants and a black shirt, and of course everybody knows that Elvis always wore black. Of course, if I wear a red shirt everybody knows Elvis always wore red. And if I wear a green suit, well only Elvis would wear a green suit. That's the way it was. The colors I wore were bright and my hair is dark black. It's not dyed. It always was that way. Anybody who was into Elvis would usually compare me to him whether they heard me sing or not.

MAG: What kind of reaction did you get on stage?

A: I remember looking at the people out there with their arms crossed, and the look on their faces was *Here it comes*. Like they were just ready to laugh! And I was just scared. I'd never sung with a group before. I just took a real big breath and I held it. I didn't know if I was going to be able to do it. I was standing up there frozen with kind of a mean look on my face. And I went—[SINGS OPENING LINES TO "BLUE SUEDE SHOES"] By the time I got that far, the microphone and the music kicked in, all of their faces had changed expressions dramatically to shock. It was amazing to see big husky grown men shocked. They almost looked scared. More scared than I was before I started singing.

MAG: When you're doing Elvis do you feel that you have become Elvis or are you always Alan?

A: I'm always Alan. It's just that I sounded like Elvis.

MAG: So you're always conscious of exactly what you're doing on stage?

A: Oh, yeah. Definitely. When I saw how shocked they were I knew that it wasn't the same reaction I'd seen other people get. I already knew how I sounded because I'd played myself on tape recorders. I would never have sung in front of anybody if I didn't know how I sounded myself because I didn't care what other people said. I knew what Elvis sounded like and unless I sounded exactly like him I wouldn't dare reproduce it in public.

MAG: What happened next?

A: I won the talent contest, and the club owner wanted me to come out and perform once a week or so. What I decided to do was put a show together. I had already found out what I needed to find out.

MAG: Other shows about Elvis were started after you began yours.

A: By the end of about six months other people did start doing shows about Elvis. These were the same type of people who used to do little bits of Elvis in their shows along with other people. But they didn't sound any more like Elvis when they did all-Elvis than when they did bits of him. But I thought they really dragged him through the mud when they tried to sing like him. One guy does *My Way* and explains to the people that in Elvis' latter years, although he still loved him, he wasn't feeling well and, anyway, this is one of his songs. And he'd do *My Way*. When I saw this guy doing that I wanted to go up and beat the hell out of him because Elvis Presley sounded stronger at the end than he ever did! His voice kept getting better, fuller

37

and stronger. He started singing higher notes than he ever did. Songs like *Hurt* proved it. The way he did *American Triology* and *How Great Thou Art*. At Elvis' very last performance he sang *How Great Thou Art, Hurt,* and My Way better than he ever did. But because people had seen pictures of Elvis overweight and because of all the stories about how he was sick—It was true. He was sick. But his *voice* was never sick.

MAG: We hear a lot of rumors about Elvis in his latter years. That he had a variety of problems. The things you usually hear people gossip about—like, that he may have been on drugs—

A: Had Elvis been on drugs he'd have been very skinny. Drugs do that to you. They louse up your appetite. They don't make you fat. Elvis was only on prescribed drugs. He was on prescribed drugs for the fact that he had a very serious blockage of the colon. You can make of that what you want. The fact that he had a blockage of the colon—what it actually was. When that happens it's usually pretty severe....

MAG: In his latter years, again, people sometimes say that Elvis' personality changed. He was said to be more withdrawn and living a very strange existence surrounded by his bodyguards.

A: Can you give me an accounting of how Elvis lived in 1957? Did he walk down the streets? Do you realize that in 1957 how if Elvis would have walked down the street for anything it would have turned the whole city that he did it in upside down? Elvis used to get chased all over the place. In 1957 Elvis was more popular than The Beatles ever could have dreamed of being. Girls would do anything to get to him—*anything!* I mean, it was not safe for him to go out in public then, and he never did. So in 1957 he was more of a recluse than he was in 1977. Graceland Mansion was built in 1957. The guards were put outside the gates in 1957. Elvis had 150 bodyguards lining the stage when he played in Los Angeles in 1957.

MAG: People have, again, put out rumors that Elvis' death was a suicide. Have you heard that and do you lend any credence to it?

A: No. Elvis didn't commit suicide. He definitely wouldn't do that the night before he was going to perform. He was planning on performing: He wouldn't have done it with his estate in the mess that it was in. As far as Lisa Marie [Elvis' daughter], he wanted her to get everything. There were other people related to Elvis who wanted to get things. Elvis knew he was dying. He knew he didn't have much time, and so did everybody else who worked with him. Most people knew, and they wanted to do what they could to get their part, their share. He was very concerned about not getting that together. Probably the biggest thing to him was making sure that Lisa didn't get cheated. These are things that I know for fact. I won't tell you my source of information, who told me any of this stuff. Except that I have met with Colonel Parker several times and with Joe Esposito, Elvis' road manager, several times. I was in continuous communication with Graceland since 1975. Paulette Williams is the secretary there who used to call me. She even came to Evansville to catch my show and get some information because they were doing a fan book club. It was done by Elvis Presley's people. It was called the *Elvis Yearbook,* and I was put in the very center of it. That was really a big thing to me. For him to do that, it was almost like being endorsed.

MAG: During the year that Elvis had already been gone there have been many people promoting various Elvis products. How do you feel about that? Does that cheapen his memory or perpetuate it?

A: I feel that if they advertise products about Elvis—his real picture of likenesses of him— I don't think that cheapens his memory at all for that stuff to be publicized. Elvis' records released on RCA—I don't believe that that hurts his image in any way because it actually shows him as he was. But for people to imitate him, that's the thing that defames his memory. I sat there in a hotel in Las Vegas watching somebody do Elvis, and I watched the rection of the people. It was kind of like, "Man, that's really the way he was. It's too bad, you know." The guy happened to look a lot like Elvis and he sang like he would expect Elvis to sing if he had just had a hand grenade go off in his back and he could barely move, and he was ready to fall into his grave. That's how he would expect Elvis to sound. When Elvis sang his last concert he sounded like he was at his peak. The only way that you can find that out is to listen to his records or my show. When I talk about him I do the song the way he did it. I don't try to cover up the fact that I can't sing like him with a whole bunch of gimmicks. I just sing it straight the way he did. Because of all that I was really considering quitting.

MAG: Why were you thinking of that?

A: I was going to quit because of a lot of stories that said I was one of the best or the best [of the Elvis imitators]. Whether I was the best or not, to me that put me at the top of a garbagepile. I didn't want to be related to them. But, then a lot of fan mail came in. I've got a stack of letters about three feet high here. Basically, a lot of it made some valid points: "Just because things don't go exactly the way you want, you can't quit;" "You said you were going to sustain his memory as long as you could;" and "You said that as long as what you do makes people happy you'd go on doing it." Those are things I've said in my show since I started it five years ago. I have to fight those people [the imitators of Elvis]. I can't just walk out. My idea at first was that if I walked out it would shame them into quitting because I was going to throw something away that meant a lot to me. But the point is, that made them really happy.

MAG: They would have just moved in and taken over your market.

A: Well, they've already moved in. But to just let them there without any defense of Elvis, without any way to show the people really what Elvis sounds like—it takes a fight on my part to do that, and that's what I should go on doing more than ever. I'll do everything in my power to show the people what Elvis sounds like. That is not an easy thing to do. I can draw Elvis fans. They come. They already know what Elvis sounds like, and they've supported me since I started because I'm an Elvis fan, too. Not because I'm like Elvis in appearance or because they can identify with me as Elvis. They identify with me as themselves, an Elvis fan. It's only when I sing that I take on any characteristics that Elvis had at all.

MAG: What characteristics of Elvis do you think accounted for his enormous popularity?

A: His voice. Because his voice is what you hear on the radio. His voice is what you hear on the records. Nobody would buy a record because of the way somebody looks. Nobody would buy a record because of the way somebody moves. You only buy a record to be able to hear a sound.

MAG: Do you think that if Elvis had been singing a different type of music that he would have gone as far even with the same voice?

A:    Of course he would have because Elvis sang fifty different styles of music since he started. He started with rock 'n roll and rockabilly. Elvis went through his first change in singing in 1956 and '57. When he sang *Heartbreak Hotel* he was rockabilly. When he sang *Hound Dog* he was strictly rock 'n roll. And when he sang *Teddy Bear* it was a boogie-woogie sound. Elvis' voice continued to change. He never stayed the same. When he sang a love song I don't see how anyone could compare his love songs to rock 'n roll. And in Elvis' latter years when he was at the peak in sound he was not singing Elvis songs. *My Way* was not an Elvis song. *How Great Thou Art* was not an Elvis song. *Hurt* wasn't an Elvis song. Very few of the songs he did were Elvis songs. It didn't matter. It was the way he sounded.

MAG:  How did you feel about Elvis as a movie performer? Did you see all of his films?

A:    Yeah, I saw all of his moves as they came out.

MAG:  They were probably not the best regarded films, although they made a great deal of money. How did you respond to Elvis as a film star?

A:    Well, every time an Elvis movie came out it was my chance to go see him. It was my chance to actually see him sing. To be able to watch him without anybody interfering, like fans screaming the way they would at a concert. In 1965 Elvis never appeared in

43

concert. Neither did he appear in concert from 1960 to '69. In all those years the only way you could see Elvis was in his movies. It made no difference to the Elvis fan what he did in the movies as long as he sang. Colonel Parker, being aware of that, realized there was no need to spend millions of dollars making big production movies when all they had to do was get Elvis up there and have him sing to a couple of girls....Elvis' movies grossed a lot of money whether the overhead was high or low. I don't think they did a lot of good for his career. I think that Elvis really had acting ability. some of his movies like *Loving You, King Creole* and *Jailhouse Rock* had a lot of good acting in them. *Blue Hawaii* had good acting, but it wasn't as much of a drama. But he sang twelve songs in it. That was the greatest thing. When I went to that movie I didn't expect that there were going to be that many songs in it. Every time he sang a song I wondered if it was the last one. From then on all I cared about after I heard him sing was hearing him sing again.

MAG: If Elvis had lived, where do you think his career would have taken him over the past year? What do you think he would have done with his life?

A: In Elvis' latter years he'd always been generous, but he was even more generous than before. It seemed that it was givng that gave him the most pleasure in life. He didn't seem to enjoy life that much himself. Personally, it wasn't very enjoyable being sick. But he did like to see other people and see him making them happy. A lot of the generous things he did he didn't want publicized. The writers of the world—the critics, skeptics and news writers—always like to find an angle behind somebody doing something. Any time they'd hear that Elvis gave a car away they would try to think of some motive other than the fact that this made Elvis feel good—to give a nobody something He didn't *always* give to the main charities, though he gave to them every year. He gave to people on the streets. He might have bought at least a hundred cars in 1976 for various people without anybody ever finding out, except once. It was found out that he bought one for a girl from Memphis. The write-ups that he got over that were enough to make you sick. No wonder he made such a big secret deal out of giving something away.

MAG: Why do you think, though, that Elvis was given to making what we would probably call very grand gestures?

A: He was a very grand person, that's why. You made grand getures because you're a grand person. You don't make grand gestures because there's something wrong with you. I think the world is really sick, you know, for somebody to do something good and all that people can think about his generosity is that there's something wrong with him. I've got to admit that there must have been something wrong with Elvis for him to be so generous to an undeserving sort, because the people really don't deserve it if they're going to turn around and slap him in the face. That's the way I feel about it, and that's one of the reasons I put my show together—to get up there and show what a bunch of jerks the press is. They're the only ones I ever heard say anything bad about Elvis. The only people I ever heard say anything bad about Elvis are people who are writers because they've got that attitude, that skeptical attitude, trying to find the thing behind the scenes. In one part of my show I say the critics thought all Elvis could do is sing rock 'n roll songs. They used to say that he covered up his [lack of] singing ability with loud drums and loud jungle beat because he couldn't sing. Even though the early part of Elvis' career was studded with over two dozen ballads, they loverlooked it. Then I would sing a song like *Don't*. It shows that if they had listened they would realize that Elvis had a hell of a voice! And when I sing *My Way* that's what I attempt to prove. Before I do *My Way* I tell the people that, "A lot of you may have heard that Elvis was sick in his latter years, and that he couldn't sing. Well, this is the way Elvis did *My Way* in his final appearance, the last time he ever sang on a stage."

MAG: Did you see a direction that Elvis' music was going towards the end of his life?

A: I guess we did. On Elvis' last albums like *Moody Blue* he did *Unchained Melody* and some different songs I'd never heard him do before. I was amazed at what he was doing with his voice. It was like he was experimenting. Then he went and died, and it just shocked me because aside from the fact that I loved him whether he was doing anything or not, it would have made no difference, it still would have killed me—but what he was doing with his voice, it seemed to me he was at his peak. He was just beginning to do something new. If you listened to his last albums you'd hear some things on there ain't never done before! He was into a falsetto sound and he was going lower in pitch than he'd ever gone. In some of his songs he would go very low, deeper than he'd sung before. At the same time in the same song he'd turn around and go into a falsetto. He did this version of *Little Darlin'*. And though the song, itself, is not that much of a song, one part of it went high and he did the falsetto part himself. You could hear that it was Elvis on that note. On *Hurt* he went really high. But on *Little Darlin'* he went twice as high. He made *Hurt* sound low when he did that. It seemed to me that he was really doing a lot of work in expanding his vocal techniques, learning new techniques and doing more things. Elvis would have just kept going up and up.

MAG: What would you say was his best work over the years?

A: It's almost like there was more than one

Elvis. It's almost like there were five of him. Because Elvis had his Best Work in 1957. He had his Best Work of the '60s. And his Best Work of the late '60s. His Best Work of the early '70s, and his Best Work of the last stage of his career. It was like they were different, but they were all his best.

MAG: Well, supposing we were going to send you off to a desert island with a stereo system, and you could only take two Elvis albums along. That's all there was room to pack. I know it would be a hard choice, but what would you take?

A: I would take *Gold Record Volume One,* which would give me songs like *Teddy Bear* and *Jailhouse Rock* and *I Want You, I Need You.* It has a good variety of his big hits of the '50s. And I would take *Elvis In Concert* because it would show how good he did the gospel songs and his latter songs like *Burnin' Love.* I would be very sorry, though, that I didn't get to take along *Gold Record Volume Three,* which was of the '60s and had *It's Now Or Never* on it, because that may have been some of his best work. But these are the two albums I would take.

MAG: 038And supposing that we had a movie theatre on the same desert island and we could show you one Elvis film. Which one would that be?

A: *Loving You* would be the film that I would want to see over and over.

MAG: Why is that?

A: Because I like the way he sang in it, and I like

**48**

the way he looked in it. And although I know everything about the movie, it's still good to see it. I've memorized the movie. I know exactly what's going to happen in it because I've seen it so many times. I rented a print of the movie myself once before and watched it over and over again.

MAG: I know that BMI [Broadcast Music, Inc., the licensing agency] has announced some restrictions regarding the use of Elvis' material. That obviously hasn't stopped you.

A: It hasn't stopped anybody. That's the problem. It isn't going to stop me because it's not intended to stop me. I wish it would stop some people. See, I pay rights—royalties—to BMI. I have an album that was recorded before Elvis died, which is fully licensed. On every song royalties are paid. They [BMI] will not issue any more licenses to anybody.

MAG: What if you wanted to record a new album of Elvis songs. Would BMI license that?

A: I don't know. I think they would license anything I did. I'm not sure. All I know is the last time I talked to Colonel Parker was when I was considering quitting right after Elvis died. I didn't feel that I could go on. I talked to him [Colonel Parker] for over a half-hour, and I talked to him again for about the same amount of time the next day. I told him that I knew that there was going to be hundreds of other people coming along. He said, "Oh, they're already here."

And I told him that I didn't think I could continue to sing with a field day being made out of Elvis' death. He told me that I should never stop, and I should go on doing it and that I shouldn't do songs other than Elvis' songs. I should just do Elvis' songs. He was very specific in what he said. He was very determined to tell me that he'd seen some of the others, and that I didn't have to worry about them because they weren't any good at all, and that they didn't even draw crowds. And that he was working on something that might stop them with his attorneys. That he was going to try to stop them. I assume that BMI was the thing that he did, though I haven't talked to him since September 1977. He told me he would be getting in touch with me, though he hasn't since I talked to him last. He figured that there was a way to set me apart from the rest so the people would know there is a tribute to Elvis, and then there is a bunch of people who are trying t capitalize on memories of Elvis and people's emotions. We haven't contacted each other yet since that time and, maybe, for all I know, he's changed his mind or forgotten. But I do know that what he said at the time meant a lot because he said as far as he was concerned Elvis was not dead That he would continue to manage Elvis because Elvis was still here—his records are still here and his product is still here and he still considers himself Elvis' manager and he wants to manage Elvis' memory. I guess that's what he meant. He seemed very sincere about what I do. I got a telegram from Elvis and Colonel Parker two years ago when Elvis was playing in Las Vegas and I was up in Canada. It extended best wishes to me about what I did. They'd just seen me on the *Donny & Marie* television show, and really appreciated it. I was invited down to see his show and to go backstage and meet him. When I got down there I think Lisa was sick and he couldn't meet me because he had to take care of her or spend more time with her.

MAG: He was very devoted to her wasn't he?

A: Oh, yeah. this reminds me that some people who imitate Elvis feel that to copy his personal life they've named their daughter Lisa. They've got a mother who looks like Elvis' mother, a daughter who looks like Elvis' daughter, and they look like Elvis. I cannot understand how that could make somebody consider himself an entertainer in any right. It's a matter of course that it's the way Elvis' mother looked. It's just a matter of the way his daughter looks. I don't think anybody could have given a damn about what she looked like or even if he ever had a daughter. it was what Elvis did onstage that made people love him. The way that he performed was his talent, his ability and his genius.

MAG: I wanted to ask you to comment about Colonel Parker. A good guessing game that people have played is would Elvis have gone as far as he did if it hadn't been for Colonel Parker. What do you think?

A:     I don't think so. It's not because Elvis wasn't good enough. But no matter how good you are you have to have the right people behind you to promote you. You have to have the right people to put you in front of the right people. Colonel Parker took Elvis from *Louisiana Hayride,* where the only people seeing him were a bunch of cowboys, to the people of the world. A lot of people at first couldn't believe that Elvis could appeal to anybody except the South. They thought he wouldn't be accepted elsewhere. But Colonel Parker knew that he would be, and he exposed him to people all over the world. And people all over the world loved him. He got RCA Records to sign Elvis, and at first they were very skeptical about him and how people would react to a white man who sounded like a black man. Back then they had black radio stations that only played black music, and white stations that only played white music. Because Elvis was white and sounded black, it looked like, maybe, the white stations wouldn't play him. And it looked like the black stations wouldn't play him because he sounded black, but he wasn't. There was a big prejudice thing then, and I think Elvis put a hole in the prejudice just because he came up with a universal sound. He mixed rhythm & blues and gospel. I think the management that he had by exposing him is what had to do with launching his career. Now once Elvis became popular I think you probably could have taken over or anybody could have. But it did take some initial work to make that country boy into a superstar.

MAG: Do you have a message for the Elvis fans everywhere who will be reading this book?

A: If I can't bring my tribute to Elvis to you— the only true tribute to Elvis that there is— they should listen to an Elvis Presley record and look at his picture. As long as they have that they have the true tribute because there's no greater tribute to Elvis than himself. Nothing can surpass him. Nothing can equal the power that he has. His charisma comes out on the records. Buy his records and listen to them.

# CHAPTER THREE

## AUGUST 16, 1977

*"I don't know what he does, but
it drives people crazy," Ed
Sullivan told the country
on National Television.*

Memphis. Tennessee. Tuesday,
August 16, 1977. The 228th day of the year.

It is 4 a.m. Most of Memphis is asleep. Over on
Elvis Presley Boulevard behind Graceland mansion,
his 18-room palace, the racquetball court lights are
burning.

The old Elvis, weight 175 pounds, could have
played a mean game of raquetball. But with 25 or 30
extra pounds hanging on that same frame he has to
drive himself harder and harder to kill the tiny ball.

He'll punish himself until about 5:30.

Racquetball, ironically enough, is a game people play to stay fit, to keep trim, to feel good and to live longer. People are going to say it's too bad it didn't work out that way for Elvis.

It is now 6 a.m. Most people are starting their day or are fast approaching it. It's going to be hot again today.

Elvis is calling it a night. He's exhausted, dripping with perspiration. He climbs the stairs to the second floor of Graceland for the last time in his life. He walks down the hallway to his master bedroom suite for the last time. Perhaps he reflects on what a far cry this stately mansion is from the two-room shack in Tupelo, Mississippi where his life began on January 8, 1935.

As he makes his way through the house, heading for his comfortable bedroom, he is not alone.

Giner Alden, Elvis' 20 year old finacee, was also staying at Graceland at the time. She was wearing a 15-carat diamond engagement ring that Elvis had given her the previous January. Set in platinum, the fabulously large diamond is surrounded by six small diamonds.

In all likelihood, Ginger was the last person to see Elvis alive and the first to see him dead. The initial reports from Memphis on August 16 were that Elvis' road manager, Joe Esposito, one of his high school buddies from way back, had discovered the body at 2:30 that afternoon. But, subsequently, it was revealed by Ginger's mother, Mrs. Jo Alden, that Ginger herself had first found the singer's corpse.

What had happened in the wee hours of Tuesday morning? After smashing a racquetball around the court for a while Elvis had gone upstairs to bed. He wasn't ready to sleep yet, but he was tired and wanted to relax. He told Ginger he was going to read in his dressing room. Ginger was tired, too. She dozed off soon and didn't awaken until close to one that afternoon.

"She knocked on the bathroom door and did not get a response," Mrs. Alden explained. "she found he had fallen out of a chair on his knees, with his face to one side and his face was purplish-red. She called for Al Strada, a wardrobe man, for help."

It is now 2:30 p.m. Joe Esposito feels for a heartbeat, but there is none. He immediately begins emergency resuscitation, but gets no response from Elvis.

Leaving the dead singer, he dashes to the telephone and calls Dr. George Nichopoulos, Elvis' personal physician. A moment later he phones the Memphis Fire Department and asks that an ambulance hurry to Graceland.

The moments seem like hours. Time has no dimension that day. The ambulance arrives, and Ulysses Jones Jr. and Charlie Crosby take over. But it was too late.

Dr. Nichopoulos hurries to Graceland. He joins the first aid team slaving over the dead singer's body. "Come on, Elvis, breathe," he cries. "Breathe for me."

But he is talking to a corpse, and there will never be any answer. Twenty-five minutes of emergency efforts bear no fruit. Dr. Nichopoulos directs Jones and Crosby to bring Elvis to Memphis' Baptist Hospital.

Minutes later Elvis is in the emergency room.

Again the best efforts of science and medicine are applied. And, again, they fail. It reminds one of the desperate emergency room work in Dallas the day JFK was assassinated. Doctors can do so much and no more. They cannot rekindle the flame of life once it has been snuffed out.

At 3:30 p.m. Elvis is pronounced dead. There is no good news to tell the world. The papers across the country and around the world can set their blackest type, their boldest letters and proclaim the end of what had started in 1956 as the *Elvis Era*. Radio and television stations throughout the United States broke the news in bulletins that many listeners and viewers simply could not believe.

How could Elvis Presley be dead? After all, he was only 42 years old. He was in the prime of life. He hadn't been sick. There had been no death watch as there had been for Groucho Marx, who died later that same week at age 86.

What killed Elvis? After an autopsy was performed, Shelby County Medical Examiner Dr. Jerry Francisco declared that the singer had died of "cardiac arrythmia." In simple language, Elvis had a very irregular heartbeat.

"There was severe cardiovascular disease present," Dr. Francisco explained. "He had a history of mild hypertension and some coronary artery disease. These two diseases may be responsible for cardiac arrythmia, but the precise cause was not determined. Basically, it was a natural death. But the precise cause of death may never be discovered."

Dr. Francisco, who is a forensic pathologist, later told reporters that he had not found anything as a result of his autopsy to substantiate rumors about

Elvis that, "paint a story of a chronic drug abuser mainlining. There were just no scars or marks to show that."

He noted that, "I cannot deny he took pills. He did." These, he said, were prescribed for Elvis' hypertension and a colon problem. "If he took pills (such as amphetamines) I have no evidence they made any kind of problem."

At the time of his death Elvis weighted over 200 pounds. "He probably was 25 to 30 pounds overweight," according to Dr. Francisco. "His weight did not produce any special strain on his heart. It probably was not any significant contributing factor. But it would have added some strain. I have no reason to think his weight contributed to his death. It becomes a peripheral possibility only."

But, he agreed, Elvis' high blood pressure could have brought about the irregular heartbeat to which death was attributed. Elvis' own doctor, Dr. Nichopoulos, revealed that his patient's blood pressure had been as high as 175 over 110 without medication.

Elvis had been under Dr. Nichopoulos' care for several years in connection with his high blood pressure problem. Like many patients, Elvis's doctor complained that he sometimes had difficulty getting Elvis to obey his medical orders.

With Elvis' death everthing changed. The wedding he is said to have been ready to announce will never take place. The road tour he was about to leave on will not happen. The managers, body-guards, business aides and associates will all have to find themselves somebody else to guide and shape and help perfect.

Elvis and Ginger were reportedly going to be married Christmas 1977. They had been considering Christmas Day, Ginger's birthday (November 13) and Elvis's birthday (January 8) as possible wedding days, according to Mrs. Alden. "They decided Tuesday on Christmas Day." Tuesday was August 16, the last day Elvis was alive.

Elvis had given the spectacular diamond engagement ring to Ginger on January 26, "but they wanted to keep it quiet until the time was right," Mrs. Alden noted. "He was going to announce their engagement Saturday night (August 27) when his tour came here (to Memphis)."

The tour that never was to be would have kept Elvis hopping for eleven days. His schedule had called for him to fly from Memphis at 11:30 p.m. Tuesday, August 16 in a private jet to Portland, Maine. The tour would have begun in Portland, where Elvis' long-time Col. Tom Parker was already at work when news came of the singer's death. The tour would have concluded with two shows in Memphis on August 27 and 28. Every scheduled show on the tour had already been sold out!

After Elvis' death ticketholders were told they could turn in their concert tickets for refunds. In Memphis many of those who held tickets for the now-canceled concerts decided against giving them up. With their refunds they would have gotten back casket had been placed very close to the front door, and there was no opportunity for mourners to get past the foyer.

The reality of the day was the dead body contained in the solid copper casket. It stood open from the top of Elvis' head to the mid-point of his chest.

The funeral itself took place the following day, Thursday, August 18, at 2 p.m. In accordance with Elvis' own wishes, the funeral was a private, family affair. The funeral procession of 49 cars was led by 11 white Cadillacs, accompanied by an entourage of motorcycle policemen. The three-mile route from Graceland Mansion to Forest Hill Cemetery was lined with anywhere from 6,000 to 8,000 mourners, depending on estimates at the time.

While crowds standing four-deep along the funeral route stood in the Memphis heat, some 200 mourners—family members, friends and business associates of Elvis—witnessed a last private funeral ceremony inside the marble mausoleum that would be Elvis' final resting place.

Elvis' copper coffin was entombed in his family's vault, which contains five other crypts, which are all empty. Elvis' mother, Gladys, to whom he was deeply attached, died in 1958.

Mrs. Presley was buried about 300 yards from the mausoleum in which Elvis' body was laid to rest. Her grave is marked with a stone that proclaimed her to be the "Sunshine of Our Home." Elvis was at the height of his popularity when she died.

Elvis' own coffin, which weighed over 900 pounds, was virtually identical to the one in which he had his mother buried. Mrs. Presley and Elvis had been so close to one another that when she passed away he was distraught. To help take his mind off the tragedy, members of the local police department are said to have taken Elvis for daily helicopter rides at the time.

half of their tickets to keep as souvenirs. But many Elvis fans decided to forego their refunds and hold on to the full tickets. A few years from now, it is predicted, the complete tickets will be worth much more than their current face value!

Just as crowds gathered to see Elvis when he was alive, they flocked to Graceland to view his dead body. About 8,000 people, many of them in tears, assembled outside the mansion's 13 acre grounds on the day after Elvis' death. Some 2,000 fans kept an all-night vigil at Graceland from Wednesday night through Thursday morning, the day of the funeral.

As if there hadn't already been a great enough tragedy, two of the teenage girls in the crowd early Tuesday morning were killed in a senseless authomobile accident. A hit-and-run driver plowed his 1963 Ford Fairlane into the crowd of mourners, killing Juanita Joanne Johnson, and Alice Hovartar, both 19.

The driver of the car, identified by police as Treatise Wheeler III of Memphis, attempted to flee from the scene of the accident. A local policeman chased Wheeler for about a block in his patrol car before forcing him to stop. Wheeler and the three girls riding as passengers in his car were the object of cries from the crowd for swift punishment. "Lynch 'em, hang him up," people were heard to demand.

Wheeler, who was 18 was tested for driving under the influence of alcohol. According to Memphis police Capt. Sam Martz of the traffic division, the test showed that Wheeler had an alcohol reading of .16. Tennessee driving laws permit a person with .10 alcohol in his blood to be charged with driving under the influence of alcohol.

When the car plowed into the crowd at about 3:30 a.m. it was traveling at 55 miles per hour. The posted speet limit was 40 pmh. The list of charges filed against Wheeler included public drunkenness, driving while under the influence of intoxicants, reckless driving, two counts of second degree murder and leaving the scene of an accident.

A third woman was seriously injured during the incident, and was identified as Tammy J. Baiter, 17, of St. Clair, Mo.

The tragic car death seemed to underscore the horrible nature of the occasion. The presence of so many thousands of dedicated Elvis fans, many of whom had driven hundreds of miles to get to Graceland, couldn't help but create a carnival atmosphere.

The event they had all turned out for was Elvis' funeral. In some ways it was said to resemble the public wake that marred the burials of Rudolph Valentino and Judy Garland years before. The fans and the police couldn't help but clash. The fans wanted to press in closer. The police wanted to keep them where they were or, if possible, push them back farther.

Repeatedly, the police announced over their bull-horns, "Try to maintain discipline if possible. There is still pushing and shoving at the front gate. If it does not stop, we will have to discontinue."

Public viewing of Elvis' body lying in state was permitted from 3-5 p.m. on Wednesday, August 17. It was estimated by police that some 25,000 people were able to enter Graceland and file past the open brass casket containing Elvis' body in the mansion's foyer.

Looking into the casket those paying their last respects saw Elvis dressed in a white suit, a light blue shirt and a dark blue tie. The suit had been a Christmas present from his father, Vernon Presley.

The weather in Memphis was hot, and the presence of so many people in a confined area made it even hotter. Many of those in the crowd couldn't take it after a while and required medical attention, themselves. There were old people, pregnant ladies and children in need of help. From time to time ambulances fought their way into the thick of things to take out the heat victims.

"Make way for the medics. We have someone on the street in need of attention," was an announcement heard often that afternoon.

It had rained earlier that morning, and low rain clouds still remained in the sky. Hot and humid weather coupled with too many people made for very unpleasant conditions.

"We have someone down north of the gate," blared one of the bullhorns.

A short while later, came the cry, "Medic, medic. South of the gate. South of the gate." With sirens wailing, the medics tried to do their best. At times it seemed that there were stretchers all over the place.

Graceland Mansion stands on Elvis Presley Boulevard. That street is normally six lanes wide. As the crowd swelled, the Boulevard was reduced to four lines, and then to a mere two. Finally all southbound traffic was stopped completely. The closest exit on the interstate highway, about a mile away, was shut so as to turn cars back.

The 25 local policeman initially assigned to crowd control in front of Graceland had to be augmented with another 25 officers. Even that wasn't sufficient. The National Guard had to be called out before the afternoon was over.

The plan had been to allow mourners in to view the body until 5 p.m. But it was clear that only a handful of those present could be accommodated during that two hour interval. An extra hour was added in a effort to give more fans an opportunity to pay their last respects.

When they finally did get inside the mansion many of Elvis' fans discovered that they had very little time to view the singer's remains. "I barely got a glimpse of him," one girl complained. "I was pushed in and out. I tried to pause long enough to look at him, but I was pushed right out."

For others, there was grim determination to get inside. "I'm going to stay until I get in," another girl declared. "I never saw him but I'm going to see him now."

Again the reminders from the police that, "Ladies and gentlemen, if you do not cooperate with the officers, we will have to discontinue. If you do not quit pushing and shoving at the front gate, we will shut the gate and discontinue. We will hve no alternative but to close the gates."

The gates of Graceland Mansion are white, with green metal guitars and musical notes as ornaments. Getting through them in the 90 degree Memphis heat was a major accomplishment. Those who did manage to get inside the house saw very little. The

It was Gladys Presley's influence on her son that made him so respectful of others that he continued to address people as sir or ma'am throughout his life. Unlike many superstars, who quickly forget their roots and think they always were on top of the world, Elvis never lost his manners.

At 2 p.m. on Thursday, August 18 private funeral services for Elvis were held at Forst Hill. Rex Humbard, the famous television evangelist, officiated. Humbard flew in from Akron, Ohio to pay tribute to Elvis, whom he had the pleasure of visiting at Graceland on a number of occasions.

Elvis pallbearers included his road manager, Joe Esposito; his personal physician, Dr. George Nichopoulos; his guitar player, Charlie Hodge; his record producer, Felton Jarvis; his friend and music publishing chief, Lamar Fike; and his cousin, Billy Smith.

Among the approximately 200 invited mourners present at the family's private funeral for Elvis were such celebrities as Ann Margaret, Bob Hope, Burt Reynolds, John Wayne, Chet Atkins, Charlie Pride and George Hamilton.

All of the mourners present at the cemetary, with the exception of Elvis' father, emerged from the marble mausoleum in about ten minutes time. When Mr. Presley did not appear, Dr. Nichopoulos hurried back into the mausoleum to see if anything was wrong. Five minutes later he returned with Mr. Presley, who had stayed behind to view the placing of his son's coffin in its crypt.

More than 25,000 floral arrangements were sent to the Presley family by Elvis' fans around the world. There simply weren't enough flowers in the city of Memphis to handle all of these orders. Flowers had to be imported from as far away as Colorado and California. In all, an extra five tons of flowers had to be flown in.

Many of the floral tributes to Elvis were inspired creations echoing themes of some of his biggest records. There were many hound-dogs made entirely of flowers. Guitars, too, were a popular subject for the florists. There was also a crown fit for a king—which Elvis certainly was in the entertainment world—made of golden mums. The effect of all of these flowers was overwhelming. The scent of flowers was everywhere, perfuming the moist, warm air. There was an extraordinary splashing of color throughout the cemetery thanks to the flowers from Elvis' admirers.

After the funeral the Presley family allowed the thousands of Elvis fans present to take the flowers as keepsakes, souvenirs of having been in Memphis for the tragic farewell to their idol. The fans were supposed to each take just one flower, but many helped themselves to armfuls of the funeral flowers. The flowers were picked clean before very long.

Elvis' death was a blow not only to his family and his fans, but also to RCA Records, the company for whom he had recorded since 1956. Unlike many rock artists, who change record labels as frequently as they change shirts, Elvis remained an RCA artist until his death. He had begun his recording career in Memphis with Sun Records which had released Elvis' first five discs. At that point RCA decided Elvis was worth taking a chance on and bought his contract from Sun for about $35,000, with a Cadillac tossed in as a bonus for Elvis.

While $35,000 was then considered to be a lot of money—and still is, to most people—it is a ridiculously small amount of money in comparison to the going rates for rock musicians. Artists today are writing record label deals running into the millions of dollars. The ironic aspect of the situation is that none of these current rock artists is likely to come close to doing the kind of business Elvis did for RCA.

How big was that business? The answer is staggering. In all, Elvis sold over six hundred million singles and LPs internationally for RCA from 1956-77. A hundred million of those sales had taken place within the last two years. He came out with 55 singles that sold a million or more copies. One of them, "Don't Be Cruel"/"Hound Dog", has already sold in excess of eight million copies. It was the biggest selling album ever.

"It's Now Or Never," which was released in mid-1960, sold 1,250,000 copies within a three week period. There have been 24 Elvis albums certified as "gold" by the Recording Industry Association of America, which means that they have sold at least a million dollars' worth. His "Blue Hawaii" album, taken from the soundtrack of the movie of the same title, sold some five million units.

As a motion picture star, Elvis appeared in 33 motion pictures. These grossed over $150 million at the box office. Elvis also did a great many live appearances. He had stopped touring in 1958 before he was drafted into the Army. He hit the road once again in 1969, doing about 15 tours a year since then. His tours generally involved about 50 evening performances, eash of which grossed an average of

$100,000. That's another $5 million annually for each of about eight years.

In all, it was estimated shortly after Elvis' death that all of his business activities for the 22 years in which he was active as an entertainer grossed over $43 billion. No, that's not a misprint. Not $43 million. $43 *billion!*

The President of RCA Records, Louis Couttolenc, and other key record label executives, Mel Ilbeman and Bob Summer, flew from New York to Memphis to attend their artist's funeral. Other RCA Records executives in Portland, Me. with Col. Parker preparing for Elvis' scheduled tour there. They, too, flew directly to Memphis upon learning the sad news. Col. Parker assisted the Presley family in making preparations for the funeral.

After the funeral many of the fans left Memphis to return to their homes. Many had come from distant parts of the country, caught up in the emotional surge to pay tribute to the recording artist they had loved for years. Others stayed behind, jamming a shopping center across the street from Graceland. Souvenirs were hawked throughout the area by salesmen eager to cash in on the singer's death.

Elvis Memorial T-Shirts were being grapped up for $5 each as quickly as they could be unloaded from their boxes. "It's a psychic thing," the salesman explained. "This whole thing is a metaphysical happening. It's Presley power."He went on to tell a reporter that, "I was going to Nashville to buy some shoes, and here I end up selling T-shirts. I didn't realize the loyalty of the Presley fans."

Others in the area were selling copies of the

Memphis newspapers. The *Commercial Appeal* and the *Press Scimitar,* for $3 or $5 a copy, depending on from whom you bought them. The papers normally sell for 15 cents a copy. But they seemed to disappear as quickly as they were printed.

"We started buying up all the papers from the machines for 15 cents each on the day that Elvis died," one of the ladies selling the over-priced papers pointed out. The value of the Memphis papers of August 17 will be considerable in years to come, making them attractive mini-investments at $3 or $5 apiece.

Bumper stickers, too, commemorating Elvis were being sold throughout Memphis. These proclaim "VISIT MEMPHIS—HOME OF ELVIS PRESLEY," and normally retail for 50 cents each. After Elvis' death the price shot up to $2. "I got ten of them and my boss told me to come back with $20," a salesman for a local tire store confessed.

Elvis Presley Boulevard was, of course, a sea of debris in the area near Graceland. Within hours of the singer's funeral the local streetcleaning department had started to sweep away the litter that had accumulated during the previous 2½ days.

Those Elvis fans trying to get out of Memphis to return home encountered massive traffic jams. Not only were there many thousands of Elvis mourners to contend with on the roads, but Memphis had also been host that week to a convention of some 16,000 Shriners. It made for absolute madness on the highways and throughout the city.

For those left behind there was much still left to do. Elvis' will had to be filed, and his enormous estate submitted for probate. On Monday, August

22 the late singer's will was read in Memphis Probate Court. The document was certified by Probate Judge Joseph W. Evans as Elvis' last will and testament.

Elvis's father, Vernon Presley, age 62, was named as the executor of his estate. Included in that estate is Graceland Mansion as well as all of Elvis' money, property, jewelry, clothing, and personal belongings and investments. The will had been prepared in March 1977, and was witnessed when Elvis signed it by his guitarist, Charlie Hodge, and his fiancee, Ginger Alden.

Who will inherit all of Elvis' money? The government will get much of it as payment for estate taxes. But there will be a great deal left over to establish a trust fund for Lisa Marie, Elvis' then 9 year old daughter by his first wife, Priscilla Beaulieu Presley. Elvis' 85 year old grandmother, Minnie Mae Presley, his father and other relatives were also named in the will.

No provision was made for Ginger or Priscilla in the 13-page will. "There are no special bequests, like giving an automobile to this one or a million dollars for that one," Judge Evans noted. "There are no percentages. It is left up to Vernon for whatever they need."

In the event that Elvis' father and grandmother are both dead when his daughter reaches the age of 25, she will receive all of Elvis' estate.

No mention of Col. Tom Parker was made in the will either. But Col. Parker will continue to represent Elvis in the future. Although Elvis is now gone, his music will live for many years, and there will be substantial royalties due to Elvis' estate from the future sales of his records.

Additional royalties will come to Elvis' estate as a result of various merchandising activities on his behalf in the future. On August 24, 1977 it was reported that Vernon Presley and Col. Parker had come to an agreement with a company called Factors Etc., Inc. for exclusive worldwide rights to all Elvis Presley merchandising. This includes everything except those items already covered by Elvis' arrangements with RCA Records.

As a result, any future sales of Elvis merchandise—like dolls, puzzles, clothing, guitars, etc.—will bring royalty payments to the Presley estate. In addition, the estate can refuse to enter into any merchandising agreements that it considers improper. For instance, if someone wanted to manufacture an Elvis toilet seat, the estate could decide that that was not a proper way to memorialize Elvis and could refuse to permit it.

Just as Elvis was a big business when he was alive, he continues to be a big business after his death. When the news of his death became known record stores around the country and throughout the world were faced with a sudden surge in requests for Elvis' records. Many key retail outlets were sold out within hours. They, in turn, put pressure on their suppliers and wholesalers for more Elvis albums.

Ultimately, that pressure came directly to RCA Records. The RCA plant in Indianapolis operates on a 24 hour-a-day basis when it needs to. It has the ability to produce some 250,000 albums or 200,000 singles each day. Some wholesalers reported that they had been promised delivery of newly pressed LPs within 72 hours of their requests.

Throughout the country the story was the same in record stores. "We sold out everything the first day after his death," the manager of one Major Los Angeles record store stated. "We don't expect to get more product from distributors because they're sold out also. All of a sudden I realized and customers realized that we took Elvis' music for granted and didn't even have one of his records at home. People want them now as collectors' items."

The manager of a record outlet near the UCLA campus in Los Angeles told a reporter, "We're ordering $4,000 worth of Elvis records. We're selling 15 to 20 copies of his various albums a day. I went through the Phonolog book and ordered 10 to 20 copies of each album. But there is a problem obtaining them. Ironically enough, we ran an Elvis special three weeks ago. At that time I had 500 records in stock which returned because Elvis doesn't sell that well in general."

In Nashville a record store manager commented, "People aren't buying one or two, they're buying five and 10."

Another Nashville record seller summed it up by saying, "We ran out the first day, bought 100 pieces Wednesday morning (August 17), which sold out within an hour and a half, and then had around 60 to 80 pieces flown in from our home office this morning, which were gone in two minutes."

In Chicago one giant downtown record shop had about 2500 Elvis albums on hand when the news of his death broke. By the day of his funeral all their shelves were said to have been picked clean by Windy City Elvis buffs.

In England there was extraordinary demand for

Elvis albums. His last single, "Way Down," and his final album, "Moody Blue," had only been released in Britain on August 1, 1977. Their sales soared after his death. An RCA spokesman in London noted, "We're merely fulfilling the demand at this stage. But contrary to some reports of our record company gloating over the sales, it should be obvious that we would much rather be selling all these records in Presley's lifetime rather than in his death."

There are some 12,000 members of the official fan club in the United Kingdom. The club's size is said to have doubled in the year prior to his death as the result of a revival of Elvis' popularity in England.

When Ed Sullivan introduced Elvis on T.V. to some 54 million viewers in 1956 he remarked, "I don't know what he does, but it drives people crazy." That statement has held true for 22 years, and gives every indication of continuing to hold true even though Elvis Presley, the King, is dead.

# CHAPTER FOUR

## EXTRA! EXTRA! READ ALL ABOUT IT!

*"ELVIS PRESLEY DEAD"*,
*headline in the Chicago Sun-Times,*
*August 17, 1977.*

The importance of an individual in contemporary American society can usually be gauged by the number of inches his obituary receives in the newspapers. An examination of the American newspapers for August 17 and 18, 1977 indicates that Elvis Presley's death was reported in the same kind of detail that the death of any king or president's passing would have been given.

Generally, the story was given the most prominent treatment of any news account on the front page that day. What else happened on August 17, 1977? The story that might have been expected to grab all the headlines was the selection by President Carter of U.S. District Judge Frank Johnson to become Director of the FBI. Another top story of the day was former President Gerald Ford's announcement that he supported President Carter's proposed Panama Canal treaty. It was also that day that Secretary of State Cyrus R. Vance's trip to Communist China was announced. And it was the day on which reports were published that Russian leader Leonid I. Brezhnev was welcoming President Carter's efforts to mend troubled Soviet-American relations.

On any other day of the year these major news developments would have dominated the newspapers, television and radio. But not on August 17, 1977. That day's newspapers throughout the United States and in many other parts of the world belonged to Elvis.

In the Arkansas *Gazette,* for instance, the headline on the Elvis story declared, "ELVIS PRESLEY DIES, ENDING LEGENDARY ROCK CAREER." A picture of Elvis from a 1974 concert accompanied the story on page one. Inside, all of page 3A was devoted to covering Elvis' death. The single bannerline read, "ELVIS PRESLEY, ROCK 'N' ROLL LEGEND WHO STARTED AS TRUCK DRIVER, DIES."

Like so many of the country's newspapers, the *Gazette* found a local angle to play in connection with the Presley story. The paper reported that in the early 1950s Elvis, while still a truckdriver, had hitchhiked to Little Rock from Memphis to sing and play guitar on a Saturday night country and western music show called "Barnyard Frolic."

Oscar Alagood, who is currently an information officer for the Arkansas State Senate, was in those days the sales manager for the local radio station that broadcast the show, which he said was "sort of a poor man's version of the Grand Ole Opry." He explained that Elvis was allowed to perform there "because of his persistence and determination to get over here."

Before he started visiting Little Rock to perform, Elvis had been appearing in his free time in Shreveport, La. on the "Louisiana Hayride" program. What was he like at the time? "He didn't have the gyrations in those days, and he had just a plain haircut," Mr. Alagood explained.

"The main thing I remember about him is that when he first started dancing on stage, doing gryations or whatever you call it, he got a lot of attention," Mr. Lynch said. He added that although Elvis didn't always get paid for appearing, "we paid him 60 bucks to come over here (once), which was a lot of money then. He did a lot for the show."

Mr. Alagood remembered that Elvis was "a very nice guy and always seemed real grateful to get on the program. He was never pushy, just nice and polite. He never gave us a bit of trouble."

In Mr. Lynch's recollection, the musicians at the time didn't think "he was all that good of a singer, but he had a lot of personality on stage. He knew how to sway the crowd. He was just full of energy, very energetic. He was out to go to the top and that's what he done."

When he came back to Little Rock a while later it

was as a major star. On May 16, 1956 Elvis did a concert there before an auditorium full of screaming fans who kept insisting, "We want Elvis. We want Elvis."

Reporting on the event the next day, the *Gazette* said that, "Elvis Presley, his guitar and his singing caused it all last night—the biggest mob scene the Auditorium had ever witnessed." The impact Elvis had in later years in Little Rock was even greater. His final concert there was on April 17, 1972 before some 10,000 fans.

The *Gazette's* critic, Bill Lewis, noted that, "It wasn't the songs that mattered. Nobody really cared about the lyrics or the melody. The persona was everything. The staccato shaking of that left leg, arched away from the right like an Indian scout's, the wildly flinging arms, the fluttering finges, the sensuous Father Earth pelvic thrusts, every gesture brought squeals of delight bordering on hysteria— just like the old days."

The Minneapolis *Tribue* carried the Elvis story under the headline, "ROCK STAR ELVIS PRESLEY DIES AT AGE 42." It was one of the more restrained accounts of his death, appearing without a picture at the bottom of the front page. Inside, however, all of page eight was devoted to the story, with the headline, "PRESLEY BECAME FOCUS FOR NEW KIND OF MUSIC ATTUNED TO NATIONS' YOUTH." Accompanying the stories were four pictures, including one of Elvis performing at a 1971 concert at Minneapolis Auditorium.

The *Tribune* carried a New York *Times* Service report by John Rockwell, which pointed out that,

77

"Bill Haley may have made the first massive rock hit, and people like Chuck Berry and Little Richard may have had an equally important creative impact on this raucous new American art form, but it was Elvis who defined the style and gave it an indelible image."

In the Tulsa *World* the story commanded the very top of page one, with the headline, "DEATH CLAIMS ELVIS PRESLEY, 42." A two-column wide photo of Elvis accompanied the report. A local angel was provided inside the paper under the headline, "ELVIS ALWAYS 'UNDISPUTED' KING FOR LOYAL TULSA FANS."

The president of the local Elvis fan club, Okies for Elvis, was quoted as saying, "The world's lost the greatest entertainer of music." Vicki Thurman went on to say, "He's gone, and there won't be another— ever. I doubt if the fan club will continue. It can't continue when the object of the club is gone."

The *World* reported that Elvis had made his first appearance in Tulsa on April 18, 1956 before over 8,000 screaming fans. There had been two performances that evening, each selling out.

Elvis returned to Tulsa again in 1972, 74 & 1976. The paper said that in 1972 the concert sold out within 17 hours. Both 1974 concerts were sold out, each with attendances of 11,575. In 1976 Elvis' appearances sold out without a single newspaper ad having to be purchased.

The 1972 concert was attended by people between the ages of 30 and 45 for the most part, the paper reported. "The kids grew up, but Presley remained their King," it said.

In Fort Worth, Texas the *Star-Telegram* devoted

most of its front page above the centerfold to the Elvis story. The main story was headlined, "ELVIS THE KING DEAD OF HEART ATTACK AT 42." Directly under that was the headline "SUPERSTAR FILLED FW SEATS."

The paper reported that Elvis made his first Fort Worth concert appearance on April 20, 1956. Although he was just getting started, 7,000 people turned out to fill the coliseum in which he appeared.

"Presley was new then. He surprised us all. He didn't wear the rumored motorcyle boots and jacket. Instead he was expensively attired in lavender sports coat, open sport shirt, black trousers and black loafers," Elston Brooks wrote.

He quoted Elvis as having said at the time, "I keep hearing rumors I'm going to die in six months. I don't know how those rumors start. I'm certainly not singing this way because I'm going to die."

In 1972, '74 and '76 Elvis returned to Fort Worth for more live appearances. They always sold out, and in 1974 his one-night concert had to be extended to four nights to accomodate the crush of Elvis fans.

The *Star-Telegram* devoted two full pages inside the paper on August 17 to pictures and stories about Elvis. One report, headlined, "FW FANS CRUSHED BY ELVIS' DEATH," quoted many local residents' reactions to Elvis' passing. Richey Davidson, who wrote an Elvis Presley Fan Club newsletter in the area, said, "We plan to have some sort of memorial, maybe show some of the film I've shot of him. My phone has been ringing off the hook with members calling from all over the country. Elvis' death will hurt the club some because most of what we wrote in the newsletter was about the concerts."

Another story recapped a prediction by seeress Jeanne Dixon, who said on July 10 that Elvis would have "recurring problems with his health. His ailments will make it difficult for him to fulfill his contracts for personal appearances." Her prediction went on to say that because his illness would keep him from working for quite some time Elvis would later try to make up for time lost by overworking himself, thereby endangering his heart.

Another wire service report quoted Elvis' fifth grade teacher, Oleta Grimes, as remembering him as "that wonderful boy" in her Tupelo, Miss. class. "People have asked me what kind of boy Elvis was and I couldn't say enough about him," she told a reporter. "And that was coming from the heart."

Mrs. Grimes claimed that Elvis had musical talent even back in grade school. "He sang 'Old Shep,' a song about a dog, in the fifth grade. He won second place at the fair on that," she recalled.

A separate local story focused on the reaction of members of an area fan club of women in their 30s called Raised on Elvis. "I'm just devastated. It's as if I lost a member of my own family," Jane Jarrell cried.

Club Vice President Tina Brazier declared, "I can't imagine my life without him. I can't even think what it's going to be like tomorrow." Club President Brenda Davidson asked, "What is there left? It's different just playing a record. I'm just glad we saw him so many times."

The Indianapolis *Star* ran the Elvis story at the top of page one with a picture and the headline, "FROM TRUCK DRIVER TO MILLIONAIRE:

ELVIS DEAD AT 42: STARTED ROCK MUSIC ERA." Inside there were a variety of pictures and stories, including one which headlined, "HOOSIER FANS MOURN DEATH OF 'THE KING.'"

Nyla Johnson, former president of an area That's the Way It Is fan club for Elvis was quoted as saying that when she attended his June 26 concert in Indianapolis, the last show on that tour, "I had the strangest feeling at the concert that I would never see him again. He just hadn't been himself lately and I think he had been sick much longer, and much more seriously, than anyone ever knew except those close to him. He was a beautiful human being as well as a top entertainer—no one will ever forget Elvis Presley."

The *Star* reported that, "Indianapolis saw a lot of Elvis in the mid-50s. He appeared there in several country music shows before his historic pelvis-swinging debut on the Ed Sullivan television show. An overnight success because of this exposure, Elvis returned to the Lyric Theatre that same year to honor a previously-signed contract."

Sheilah Craft, a 15 year old Indianapolis fan of Elvis, was quoted as saying, "I can't believe it. I just can't believe he's gone. He should have taken better care of himself."

The Arizona *Republic* in Phoenix played the Elvis story near the top of page one with a large two-column picture and the headline, "ELVIS PRESLEY DIES AT 42: ERRATIC HEART-BEAT BLAMED." Inside the paper, all of page A-16 was devoted to Elvis, complete with three photos, two of which ran three columns wide.

One of the inside stories about Elvis was

headlined, "FEARS MADE PRESLEY 'A HAUNTED MAN.'" The story, from United Press International, quoted singer Pat Boone as saying that Elvis "was a haunted man almost necessarily. I felt sorry for him because when I visited him, I thought I was visiting an exile of some kingdom.

"He didn't go out and expose himself to the general public in the street. If he wanted to see a movie, he'd hire the theatre and a projectionist and allow only friends inside.

"When he started gaining weight, he wondered whether he still had it as a performer."

Boone and Elvis first met in Cleveland during the mid-1950s. They appeared together at the time, but it was Pat who was the headliner. Elvis was still not a superstar, and was merely the show opener. "We shook hands after the show," Boone recalled. "He seemed bashful, withdrawn and unassure of himself. But he had a fantastic impact on the audience and from there on we seesawed back and forth on the music charts."

What about the reports years ago that Elvis and Pat were feuding? "We were actually the best of friends," he was quoted as saying. "That whole thing about us feuding was just drummed up by the media and we laughed together about it."

According to Pat Boone, Elvis "died young like James Dean and perhaps that's the best way for the public to remember him. No one can imagine an old Elvis."

In another story, from the Associated Press, it was reported in the *Republic* that officials of the Hilton Hotel chain were shocked by Elvis' sudden death. "There will never be another Elvis Presley,"

Barron Hilton, head of the chain, was quoted as saying.

In recent years Elvis had performed exclusively at the chain's Las Vegas Hilton. He had been the second performer—after Barbra Streisand opened it—to appear at the hotel when it first opened in 1969 as the International under a different management. His annual engagements at Christmas were always sold out weeks in advance.

"We are deeply shocked and saddened at the loss of this outstanding superstar," a spokesman for the hotel told reporters. "Elvis Presley was more than just a great talent. He was a good friend of all of us at the Las Vegas Hilton. He was most certainly the world's top entertainer and he will be greatly missed by all of us."

Elvis' physician in Las Vegas, Dr. Elias Ghanem, was quoted as saying, "He was never sick, really. He just had a sore throat once in a while. But that's about it. he was always in perfect health." The doctor also revealed that he had examined Elvis last March for insurance purposes and had found him to be in fine health.

In nearby Tucson, the Arizona *Daily Star* ran the Elvis news as the top story on its front page. There were four pictures of Elvis above the headline, "ELVIS HEART VICTIM." In a separate story headlined "MEMORIES SELL FAST" the paper reported on the reactions of Tucson fans.

Elvis had made his first appearance in Tucson in 1956, and had been back again in 1972 and 1976. John Cristison, assistant director of the arena at which he had last appeared, recalled that, "He didn't look well. He looked tired. I think it's a loss to everyone. I don't know how old you are, but I grew up with the guy. He was a phenomenon that will never come again. It's sad. He could have come back for 10 years and still packed the house."

Police Sgt. Rick Milne had worked as Elvis' driver during his last Tucson appearance. "It's a shame. He was a great entertainer," he commented. "He was a very quiet individual. He came here from a concert in El Paso. He was extremely tired, and didn't talk much."

But Elvis was always thoughtful when it came to those who worked closely with him. Before leaving Tucson he gave Sgt. Milne a scarf to take home to his wife. It was the same type of scarf that Elvis frequently tossed to his screaming fans at his concerts.

The Daily *Star's* story mentioned, as a number of other newspaper accounts in other cities did, too, that when Elvis made his 1976 appearance he did not allow any reporters or photographers to get close to him. He was surrounded by bodyguards, and was noticeably overweight. Still, he continued to do sell-out business in Tucson and, apparently, everywhere else, too.

The Sentinel *Star* in Orlando, Florida devoted the top half of its front page to Elvis. The paper ran a color photograph of Elvis across six columns, under an eight column banner line, "ELVIS: THE KING IS DEAD." Inside, all of page 5-A was devoted to Elvis.

The Sentinel *Star* reported that when Elvis last appeared there on February 15, 1977 he didn't appear to be at the top of his form. "He looked so bad," one woman was quoted as saying. "He looked tired and sick. And the way he couldn't stay with the band, it just wasn't the same."

After that concert one Orlando critic wrote that Elvis had "tried to make up with his eyes what he no longer had in the pelvis." Still, his impact was substantial. A woman cried after the concert, "Dear God, he's the king and I didn't even get to touch his scarf. If only I could have touched it."

As in so many other cities, Elvis' albums sold like hotcakes in Orlando after his death. One woman, Catherine McGuinness, bought $230 worth of his LPs, explaining, "I loved him. He was fantastic. He was so down to earth." The manager of a large record store reported having sold over 200 Elvis LPs the night after his death, including all copies of "Moody Blue," Elvis' last album. Like record outlet managers everywhere he was trying to get more albums from RCA to meet local demand.

The Sacramento *Bee* in Sacramento, Calif. splashed the Elvis story over much of its front page, under the headline, "HEART AILMENT KILLS ELVIS. FANS MOURN FOR A KING OF ROCK 'N' ROLL." There were four one-column head shots of Elvis, showing how he had changed from 1957 to 1977. The puffiness in the face, the extra weight, the double chin and the drawn, tired look were readily apparent. Not a word had to be said for the reader to get the message. Elvis was a long way from where he had started.

An inside story in The *Bee* was headlined, "SHOCKING DISBELIEF FILLS MINDS OF ELVIS FOLLOWERS." The report from UPI quoted actress Ann-Margret, who co-starred with Elvis in the film "Viva Las Vegas," as saying, "I have lost a very dear friend and the world has lost a very great entertainer."

Disc jockey Wolfman Jack, who appeared in the movie "American Graffiti," declared that Elvis would "go down in history. Two thousand years from now, you'll still be hearing about Elvis Presley."

A fan of Elvis' in Denver, Ellen Levine, put it very well when she cried, "I just thought he was going to be around always. I just don't know what it's going to be like without Elvis in the world anymore."

Another fan, Marci Loeser of Memphis, said, "My first reation was disbelief. I couldn't believe it. I asked other people and they couldn't believe it either."

Another Memphis fan, Maribeth Peagram, confessed, "It's almost like when my mother died."

In Madison, Wis. Keith Lowry, Jr. was quoted as saying, "I felt like one of my own family died."

In much of the nation's press coverage of Elvis' death that same theme can be found. The fans couldn't believe or accept the news as being true, although they quickly discovered that no one was pulling their leg. Also, the fans felt as though a member of their own family had died. Elvis was very close to them.

Elaine Sharp, an assistant manager for the telephone company in Memphis, reported that, "We have received calls from all over the world—Japan, Europe, Australia. People were calling to express their loss. Their loss and heaven's gain."

The New Orleans *Times-Picayune* ran a large photo of Elvis at the top of its front page, above the headline, "HEART ATTACK KILLS ELVIS AT AGE 42." The paper devoted all of its second page to reports on Elvis.

In one fascinating account about local reaction to the singer's death, nightclub owner Lois Brown was quoted. She recalled having refused to hire Elvis back in 1954, "because he wasn't well-known enough."

She explained that, "In 1954 Keith Rush booked Elvis for $150 a night at my place, the Cadillac Club on St. Claude Avenue. Keith said 'he's a real hot number.' Well, we didn't take him—and I still regret it—but since then we became very good friends. We hired the Everly Brothers instead."

Elvis' debut in New Orleans was delayed until August 12, 1956, when he did two concerts at Municipal Auditorium. Walter Taney, who handled that booking, was quoted as saying that Elvis was "one of the nicest young men you'd ever want to meet. It was 'Yes, Ma'm' and 'Yes, Sir' to older people."

Tickets in those days weren't anything like today's prices. Orleanians were able to buy their way into the auditorium for $1.05, $1.26 and $1.47 depending on location.

The local critics weren't sure what to make of Elvis. One of them wrote at the time. "Whether he'll be around as long as the Davy Crokett hat remains to be seen. He flings his limbs about and quivers in such a way as to make one think he might have a trick knee, possibly from an old war injury. But this is not the case."

Elvis returned to New Orleans in 1958 for the filming of his movie, "King Creole," which was set in the famous French Quarter of the city. By them he was a superstar, and mobs of teenagers followed him around.

Elvis is said to have liked New Orleans very much. He became friendly with Lois Brown, and visited her there many times. "We'd see him at least once a year—every time he came here," she pointed out. "He was one of the sweetest guys this side of heaven."

In another *Times-Picayune* story reporter Joe Massa shared with his readers his memories of having been in the Army with Elvis. He revealed how he and eight other recruits had been selected in 1958 to follow Elvis through his military career and report on his comings and goings for the benefit of the folks back home. This was all part of a public relations campaign devised by the Army to take advantage of Elvis' presence in its ranks.

What sort of person was Elvis? "He was aloof, but not in a rude sort of way," Massa wrote. "Throughout his Army hitch, Elvis was congenial, but of few words. He was friendly, with a ready smile for practically anyone."

The death of his mother may possibly have been a reason for this, according to Massa. "It apparently affected him deeply and may have accounted for his somewhat solemn personality, quiet, reflective and—to put it briefly—set apart though one of us."

The Chicago *Sun Times* carried the simple headline "ELVIS PRESLEY DEAD" in its early edition of August 17. The news hit too close to press time to get anything inside the paper, or even to get a picture of Elvis on the front page. But the early Asssociated Press report from Memphis was splashed across the tabloid's page one. Later editions carried the story in detail.

The Los Angeles *Times* devoted a substantial amount of space to the Elvis story. Three pictures ran on the front page above the headline "ELVIS PRESLEY DIES AT 42: LEGEND OF ROCK 'N' ROLL ERA." A second story also ran on page one in which the paper's pop music critic, Robert Hilburn, provided an analysis of Elvis' music.

In his story Hilburn quoted Phil Spector as having once said during a late Elvis performance in Las Vegas, "Hey, he's doing us a favor being up on that stage. He may be overweight, and he may not move like he used to, but he doesn't have to be there. He doesn't need the money. We're lucky to be able to see him. Some day we're going to say, "Damn, I wish I could still see him."

In another account, The *Times* quoted a number of Elvis' fans and friends in Memphis. Gov. Ray Blanton of Tennessee was said to have called Elvis, "the greatest talent this country, maybe the world, has ever produced."

Charles Foren, who owns a Memphis nightclub called The Vapors, observed that, "I remember Elvis. A nice kid."

Another friend insisted that Elvis wasn't actually fat, but that "It was just water, bloat from medication he took."

Fred Stoll, who had been Elvis' gatekeeper at Graceland for the past 14 years, commented, "I just saw Elvis early this morning. He smiled and waved. He looked good to me." He also noted that while Elvis was alive, "It wasn't unusual for 30 to 50 people to be gathered at the gate here."

The Albuquerque *Journal* ran a three column photo of the crowds outside Graceland on the front page of its edition of Thursday morning, August 18. The headline read, "MORE THAN 75,000 MOURNERS SEEK LAST GLIMPSE OF PRESLEY." The story, taken from the wire services, reported that Elton John, the British rock superstar, had sent a floral arrangement that now stood before the gates to Graceland. The card on it simply said, "For all the inspiration."

A statement by President Carter was quoted, proclaiming that Elvis' death "deprives our country of a part of itself. His music and his personality, fusing the styles of white country and black rhythm and blues, permanently changed the face of the American popular culture."

An unnamed "British pop star" was said to have commented that, "If there had been no Elvis, there would have been no Beatles."

A 40 year old woman from nearby Jackson, Tenn., Ann Smith, told reporters, "He's the king, and he has been for 20 years. I just had to come." She came with her mother and her three daughters, and had been waiting for about six hours when she was interviewed!

This was typical of the coverage of the Elvis story onthe second day, August 18. Many papers had already run detailed feature stories about Elvis the previus day. Those that had not caught up with the news on the 18th. In some cities the papers continued to play up the story on the front page for several days, with additional features inside every day. Clearly, the readers wanted every bit of information coming out of Memphis.

The Portland *Oregonian* carried an August 18 story on its front page, at the bottom, headlined, "FEW ABLE TO VIEW BODY OF PRESLEY: PRIVATE FUNERAL PLANNED." In another story the paper reported on a unique "Tribute to Elvis' performance in Longview, Wash.

The tribute had been scheduled as a week long engagement by singer Johnny Rusk prior to Elvis' death. Many of Elvis' best fans in the area, mostly women in their 30s, were on hand for the show. One of them, Laura Lefebvre, recalled how she had seen Elvis at the Seattle World's Fair when she was just 15. "At the fair I got right next to him and asked him if I could have his can of pop when he was done," she said. "He handed it to me. I still have it. My husband hides the can just to make me mad, but then I threaten to burn his Tammy Wynette record."

She added, "Last November in Portland, he was throwing scarves off the stage and a lady got one, and two guys grabbed both ends and pulled. She was actually choking. I told them to let go and they did. Then I told her to run out of there and stuff the scarf fown her blouse because they'll try to get it again."

Mrs. Lefebvre is so devoted an Elvis fan that she still carries in her wallet the ticket stubs from the four Elvis concerts that she attended in the past. A survey of the nation's press indicates that there are many others just like her everywhere.

The paper also quoted Ken Evans of Provo, Utah, who was in the 81st Armored Division at Ft. Hood, Texas with Elvis. "I got cold chills whenever I got around that man," he explained. "He had a heart of gold...donated thousands of dollars to an entertainment center at the camp."

Still another article in The *Oregonian* focused on Elvis' music. Carl Wilson of The Beach Boys was quoted as saying, "His music was the only thing exclusively ours. His wasn't my mom and dad's music." John Lennon, the ex-Beattle, once said that, "Nothing really affected me until Elvis."

Col. Parker, quoted in the same story, noted that, "When I found Elvis, the boy had nothing but a million dollars worth of talent. Now he has a million dollars."

Commenting on Elvis' passing in an editorial, The *Oregonian* summed it up this way. "His death at age 42 is a painful reminder to his middle-aged fans of the 1950s and their elderly parents that rock 'n' roll, that loud amalgam of both real and contrived folklore and spiritual music that once shocked the world, is now more than 25 years old. But even those who censored Elvis and his grinding, bumping hips in the mid-1950s must now feel a deep nostalgia and sadness that their children's golden idol is dead."

The Dallas *Times Herald* devoted considerable attention to the Elvis story in its editions of Thursday evening, August 18. The top story on the front page was headlined, "CAR SLAMS INTO PRESLEY MOURNERS, KILLS 2." There was a dramatic three column photo of people giving first aid to one of the injured women. Inside were a number of stories, one of which dealt with how Elvis' fiancee, Ginger Alden, and not his road manager as originally reported, had first discovered his dead body.

Another *Times Herald* story reported on the sad fact that Elvis never got to see a $40,000 van that had been customized in his honor. "It's just a shame," Robert O'Brien, President of the company that prepared the custom van said. "Here's this guy who loved cars, loved 'class' and only wanted to be involved with winners and number one. This van just won first place in the Nationals in Pennsylvania over the weekend, and we brought it down here (to Memphis) because Col. Tom Parker had told us Elvis would want to see it. And the guy went to his grave without getting to see this thing and how people appreciate it."

The van is painted hot pink and black on the outside, and has a rear tire cover bearing a portrait of Elvis. It's called Heartbreak Hotel, and boasts a refrigerator stocked with what O'Brien said was Elvis' favorite pink champagne.

"We truly, sincerely did it out of wanting to build it to be a tribute to him. And I'm going to stop showing it for several months as kind of a mourning period for Elvis," he told a reporter.

In another story, staff writer Marie Elson interviewed a number of Dallas area residents who knew Elvis before he became famous. One of them, Bob Sullivan, was the recording engineer for the Louisiana Hayride show in Shreveport during the mid-1950s. It was 1955 when he first met Elvis.

"He was an exceptionally handsome kid, and we'd be sitting in a booth drinking coffee, and women would just turn around and start staring at him," Sullivan explained. "They'd be with their boyfriends or husbands, and some of those guys would come over and say, 'Hey, what are you doing flirting with my wife or my girl?' And Elvis wasn't doing anything. He was just drinking coffee and talking to me."

Sullivan said that in 1956 when Elvis returned to Shreveport for a concert, "We thought, shoot, he'll come by the station and talk. But we didn't even see the guy. That was our first contact with big time show business.

In all of the comments to be found in the stories about Elvis that appears to be the only one with anything negative to say about Elvis.

Some of the other people interviewed for the same article had candid observations regarding Elvis' talent in the early '50s. "Smokey" Montgomery, a local banjo picker and producer, is 64 years old. He first saw Elvis at the Big D Jamboree in Dallas in the '50s. "I hate to say this, but after Col. Parker took him over and I heard RCA was giving him a $50,000 advance, I thought, 'Man, RCA's got the craziest people I've heard of—they've blown their stacks.' God, how wrong could I be? I didn't even take any pictures of him when he played at the Jamboree. I saw both him and Buddy Holy perform there, but I didn't get pictures of either of them."

Sullivan also said, "You know, everybody's coming out now and saying they knew Elvis was going to be a star. But I never heard a soul say that kid wasn't nothing but a flash in the pan."

Ray Winkler, who wrote the title song on "Welcome To My World," Elvis' last LP, was working for a radio station in Amarillo, Texas in 1955. His station manager asked him to try to find a record to play on the opening program of the new radio station by "a guy named Elvis Presley."

Winkler told the paper, "I went to this record store and asked if they had any records by Presley, and they said they'd never heard of him. They said all the records they weren't interested in were down in a bottom drawer. So I looked through the drawer until I finally found a record by Elvis. I went back to the station and put it on, and it just tore the town up."

The paper's extensive Elvis coverage also included an interview with Rick LoRanc, who performs as "Rick Presley" and does an imitation of the late singer.

LoRanc noted that he was being besieged with offers to do television appearances and magazine interviews now that Elvis was dead. "Why are all these people wanting to see me now?" he questioned. "They didn't want to see me before."

He confided to the reporter that he's the best imitator of Elvis around today, "but God, let me state it very firmly. There will not be, whether it's me or anybody else, anybody who will replace that man. He's the king. The only thing I can possibly do is bring Elvis Presley into people's lives who didn't get a chance to see him.

"I'm leery of doing Elvis Presley now that he's gone. I will only do it if the public wants it. I feel very much alone without Elvis. Even though I never got to meet him, when he was here I felt better. But now that he's gone, there's an eeriness about it you'd have to be me to understand." The 27 year old performer has been doing his Elvis act since 1975, when he resigned a position he then held with IBM in Dallas.

"In my eyes, he was the greatest entertainer that ever was," LoRanc added.

The Dallas *Times Herald* also commented on Elvis' death in an editorial. The paper reflected that

"The 1950s for most adult Americans are the nostalgia years to which they can relate. The contrast between that time and today is so pronounced—with so much having happened to American culture in between—that Mr. Presley was for many persons a link to the past more than to the future."

Columnist Brian Woolley pointed out that, "There was nothing philosophical about his music. Unlike many who would follow the path that he cleared, he had no protest to make, no social message to convey. The lyrics of most of his songs didn't even make sense, and his friend Pat Boone could have crooned them forever without furrowing parental brows."

Even the paper's society columnist, Julia Sweeney, focused on Elvis. Her column that evening was headlined, "THE SUBJECT WAS ELVIS AT POST-MUSICAL PARTY." She quoted Mr. E.D. (Margaret) Rodgers as recalling her meeting with Elvis in 1956 when she was working in the Dallas Music Hall's office. She had been sent "out to the airport in a Cadillac to meet Elvis. I took two of the girls from the office with me, but I was scared to death. I don't know why, but I was.

"Well, he was just as sweet and nice as could be. I called him 'Elvis,' but he called me 'ma'am,' (and I wasn't that much older than he was). He sat on the back seat of the car between the girls and hardly said a word. He just sat there singing and humming, 'Love Me Tender' in a low voice. We asked him about Natalie Wood, and he said, 'She'll never marry Tab Hunter.' "

Of all the papers surveyed, The Dallas *Times*

*Herald* seems to have provided the most in-depth coverage of Elvis, emphasizing local angles, on the second day of the tragic news story.

The Salt Lake *Tribune's* August 18 editions carried two front page stories about Elvis. One. headlined "ELVIS FANS FROM PERU TO PAREE IN MOURNING," described the world-wide mourning for the dead star. The other story headlined "75,000 FILE PAST BODY OF PRESLEY," was a pre-funeral account from Memphis.

In an editorial The *Tribune* commented that, "Elvis Presley, himself, suffered the cruelty of his occupation—shouldered aside, almost forgotten as newcomers capitalized on the markets he and his promoters discovered. But he was proving his durability, with sell-out concerts and a new hit record, a country single: 'Way Down.' It might have been Elvis on top again if he hadn't been fatally stricken."

In its world wide mourning report the paper quoted Jimmy Savile, the British disc jockey, as saying, "Elvis was one of the few people in the world who actually did nothing but bring pleasure into the lives of people."

The French paper *Le Monde* ran a front page tribute to Elvis, noting that, "He woke up America of the '50s, but 20 years later the silent majority reclaimed him."

The Omaha *World Herald* ran a four column wide photo on its front page of the car accident outside Graceland. Inside, all of page 11 was devoted to stories about Elvis. Another inside story dealt with a three year old, Charlie Benish, of

Dallas, who is being groomed by his mother as Elvis' successor. The youngster has already been trained to gryate to Elvis' music, and his mother has high hopes that he will someday take over where Elvis left off.

The London *Observer* reported in its editions of August 21 on the front page that the Elvis Presley Fan Club of Great Britain held its scheduled convention in Nottingham despite their idol's death. The story was headlined, "PRESLEY PARTY ENDS IN WAKE." One club member, David Kaye, was doing an imitation of Elvis, and explained, "Elvis wouldn't want us to be sad today. Our kids will love Elvis songs, and their kids, and their kids again—probably forever."

Elvis' death came too late in the week for him to make the cover of either *Time* or *Newsweek*. Both magazines, however, did carry features with color photographs about his passing. The *Time* story was headlined. "LAST STOP ON THE MYSTERY TRAIN." *Newskweek's* headline was simply, "ALL SHOOK UP."

The *Time* story by Jay Cocks quoted Rod Stewart's reaction. "I am very sad," he said. "His death is a great loss to rock 'n' roll." Another rock star, Brian Wilson of the Beach Boys, said, "His music was a great inspiration t us. His personality was a great inspiration to us. He was a fine gentleman."

*Newsweek's* story by Maureen Orth quoted a blond secretary said to have known Elvis in Las Vegas, who said the singer had once taken a gun and shot the screen of his hotel room television set. "He told me it was OK because the hotel always put it on his bill," she explained. "Toward the end, though, he was paranoid. He kept in his Bible the police report of two guys who tried to rush him on the stage in 1973. My purse was always searched for weapons before I could go into his suite, and once when the cork of a champagne bottle was popped he ducked for cover and his bodyguards completely surrounded me."

In a second *Newsweek* story called "THE HEARTBREAK KID," Jack Kroll appraised Elvis' impact on American society. "When Elvis exploded, kids were no longer just individual appendages on millions of American families," he wrote. "Rock 'n' roll fused their sensibilities—and their pocketbooks—together with the white heat of the music. A tribe was born."

The coverage of Elvis' death continued for days afterwards. With the perspective of a few days, music critcis and followers of the contemporary rock scene retired to their typewriters and filled column upon column of newspaper and magazine type with comments about Elvis. For the most part, the analyses of Elvis' role in American popular culture were right on the target.

So many newspapers and magazines focused on Elvis' death that it became difficult to absorb all of the details that were suddenly brought out. The senses became flooded with input about Elvis. In many cases there were minor differences in various reports about the same events. For instance, were there 75,000 people lining the streets of Memphis, or were there 80,000? Did 200 people attend the private funeral service or were only 150 people present? Was Elvis pronounced dead at 3:30 p.m. or at 3:50 p.m.?

Did Elvis wear a dark blue tie or a white tie in his coffin? Does Graceland Mansion occupy 13 acres of land or is it on 14 acres?

None of these points is really important. Most of these figures are estimates, and they will vary depending on whom you talk to. The newspaper and wire service reporters on the scene in Memphis had to work against the clock on a tragic story of enormous proportions. They are to be commended for a job well done, for a fine final tribute to Elvis.

# CHAPTER FIVE

## ELVIS — FROM RAGS TO RICHES!

*"His death deprives our country
of a part of itself," President
Carter proclaimed.*

It is the American dream from rags to riches.
From obscurity to instant fame. From poverty to
power. From the bottom of the heap to the top of
the world.

It happened to Elvis. From time to time lightning
strikes and the American dream makes itself felt on
an individual. In the '40s it was a poor, skinny kid
from Hoboken, New Jersey, who called himself
Frank Sinatra. In the '50s it was a youngster named
Elvis Presley with sideburns and a ducktail haircut
from Tupelo, Mississippi. In the '60s it was a group
of four mop headed lads from Liverpool, England,
who called themselves The Beatles. In the '70s it will
happen to somebody else. Perhaps even to you.

Our society needs its Elvis Presleys to survive.
They give the rest of us hope that something can
happen without warning that will transform our
lives and make us happy. Of course, the happiness
never really comes as part of the package. Fame and
fortune go hand in hand, but the more we learn
about someone like Elvis the less likely we are to
believe that he was happy.

The price that someone like Elvis pays for all the
glory and the enormous salaries and having his
picture up there on the movie screens is isolation,

desolation, frustration and inundation by his fans. It is the fans who are the power brokers. They make the American dream come true when they bestow their blessings on a performer. But they also turn out to be carnivores. Sooner or later they eat their idols alive and spit out the picked-clean bones when they're through with them.

Elvis was born in a two room frame house in the poor town of Tupelo, Miss. on January 8, 1935. His father, Vernon, was a farm worker then—cotton and sugar being the local crops—and later became a factory toiler. His mother, the former Gladys Smith, had just given up her job running a sewing machine in a Tupelo clothing factory. Her work week of six days, each of at least 12 hours, was no way to prepare for bringing a healthy child into the world.

On January 8, in the early afternoon Elvis Aron Presley was born. About an hour later his twin brother, Jesse Garon, arrived. Jesse died shortly afterwards. The twins had been given rhyming names because Mrs. Presley thought that would be nice. After Jesse's death, she never had another child.

Elvis attended Lawhon Elementary School in Tupelo, where he started singing at a young age. A song he was particularly fond of was called "Old Shep," and dealt with a dog of the same name. Elvis sang that in class on occasion. As a result, he was entered in the 1945 Mississippi and Alabama Fair and Dairy Show, where he discovered that he wanted to go into show business.

At the fair Elvis sang "Old Shep," and captured second prize. He was paid the then handsome sum of $5. As a bonus, he got some free tickets to the amusement rides at the Fair.

Oleta Grimes, who had been Elvis' fifth grade teacher, was interviewed shortly after his death. She recalled him as being a "wonderful boy." Mrs. Grimes told a reporter that, "People have asked me what kind of boy Elvis was and I couldn't say enough about him. And that was coming from the heart."

The Chairman of the Elvis Presley Birthplace Restoration, Billy Boyd, told reporters after Elvis' death that Tupelo residents always regarded Elvis as a hometown boy who succeeded. "There are plenty of people who remember him as a child," she was quoted as saying. "I knew his health wasn't good, but I had no idea this would happen."

Elvis' old two-room house had been turned into a tourist attraction. "We opened in June of 1971 and we have about 7,000 to 8,000 visitors each summer," Mrs. Boyd noted. They have the opportunity to seeing the bedroom in which Elvis was born. It's the front room of the house. The bed in which Elvis arrived was an old fashioned iron bestead with a mattress that had seen better days. The floor it stood on was totally bare.

Tupelo also has its own 35 acre park in honor of Elvis. Money for that and the restoration of his old house came from a 1958 benefit concert by Elvis.

When Elvis was 11 years old his father bought him his first guitar. It cost all of $12.95, which doesn't sound like much today but represented a lot of money for a factory worker in 1946. There have been varying accounts as to whether Elvis had wanted the guitar or a bicycle as his Christmas present that year. Some reports say that Elvis had picked the guitar because it cost about four times less than the bicycle did. Other stories maintain that Elvis really wanted the bike but was given the guitar instead.

In any event, every account seems to agree that he thoroughly enjoyed the guitar once he got it. His mother was once quoted as saying, "He liked the guitar the best of all his things. He'd sit in front of the radio, picking out melodies, or sometimes he'd play the phonograph trying to learn the songs he heard." The guitar and Elvis became quite inseperable. Wherever Elvis went, the guitar did, too.

What type of music did Elvis come into contact with in those days? Well, he probably listened to the "Grand Ole Opry" radio program. Everybody did. There were records out by such white country musicians as Roy Acuff, Eddy Arnold, Jimmie Rodgers and Bob Wills. Two white gospel groups that appealed to him were the Blackwood Brothers and the Statesmen Quartet. As for rhythm and blues artists, there were Billy Eckstine, Bill Kenny and The Ink Spots.

"I dug the real lowdown Mississippi singers, mostly Big Bill Broonzy and Big Boy Crudup," he once told an interviewer, "although they would scold me at home for listening to them."

In 1948 when Elvis was 13 his family picked up and moved to Memphis, Tenn. "We were broke, man, broke, and we left Tupelo overnight," he later recalled. "Dad packed all our belongings in boxes and put them on top and in the trunk of a 1939 Plymouth. We just headed for Memphis. Things had to be better."

The Presleys had no grand illusion at the time. "We didn't have no big hopes of finding those

Memphis streets paved with gold," he once explained. "All we new, and I remember it well, was that wherever we went it sure had to be better than life in Tupelo."

Memphis was the home of much musical activity—chiefly hillbilly and blues—when the Presleys hit town. There were plenty of opportunities for Elvis to hear the latest black records. Radio station WDIA in Memphis called itself the "mother station of the Negroes" and broadcast records by B.B. King, Rufus Thomas and others. Beale Street in Memphis was a center for blues singers, as was W.C. Handy Park. Elvis' musical education had taken an important new direction.

As for his general education, he enrolled in L.C. Humes High School. He confessed to a reporter once that he was very nervous about entering the new school, and "I felt like the hair on my head was standing straight up through sheer fright." Memphis was, after all, the big city. Elvis was a country bumpkin, by comparison, and was afraid that the other kids would laugh at him. He sounded different than they did, and he didn't dress as well either.

The Presleys were just getting by in Memphis. They lived in a run-down apartment on Poplar Avenue at first, and were later allowed to move int a public housing project called Lauderdale Courts. There they enjoyed the luxury of a two bedroom apartment, which was decorated much nicer than their old place had been. The rent was about $30 a month.

Vernon Presley was working in a tool factory at the time. Gladys was earning extra money by waiting on tables in a local diner. She also worked as a nurse's aide at Baptist Hospital, where Elvis was to be pronounced dead on August 16, 1977.

Elvis had no clearcut goals as a youth, but he did tell an interviewer once that he had only hoped "to be somebody and to feel like somebody."

In his high school days Elvis was far from a leader. He was not an outstanding student, and he never did anything to distinguish himself. He played some football, enrolled in the ROTC program, and majored in history, English and manual training or shop. He wore long hair during a period when most boys wore theirs short. His sideburns—which became his trademark later in life—were originally grown because he wanted to look older and be taken for a truck driver. He was a member of his school's History, English and Speech clubs.

"Nobody knew I sang, I wasn't popular in school, I wasn't dating anybody," he once put it. "In the 11th grade at school they entered me in another talent show. I came out and did my two songs and heard people kinda rumbling and whispering. It was amazing how popular I was in school after that."

But accounts of Elvis' life question how truthful a statement that really was. It's been suggested that Elvis sought to alter history by surrounding himself after his success with many of the very people who were popular in high school but refused to even talk to him back then. He made it look like he has always been part of the same crowd, which reportedly was not the case.

His efforts to blend into Memphis high school society were considerable at the time. He tried, for example, to dress the way the other kids did. Flashy clothing, later in his life, also became an Elvis trademark. It probably compensated for the years when he didn't have the money to dress in what was considered high style in Memphis.

In 1953 Elvis was graduated from high school. Before graduation he was working at Loews State Theatre as an usher for five hours a night, earning about $13 a week. After graduation he went to work for the Precision Tool Company in Memphis. From there he joined Crown Electric Company as a truck driver, earning some $35 a week.

Working was very important to Elvis and to his family. In his high school days he had tried to work an impossibly difficult schedule. Between his studies, his movie ushering at night and his afternoon work at another point in a metal factory he was barely able to keep his eyes open. He had to quit working, his parents insisted. The family needed the money, however, and Mrs. Presley then went to work at Baptist Hospital to replace the dollars Elvis was no longer able to bring in.

The Presleys faced a problem as a result. Their combined income was now in excess of the amount that families could make and still live in the low-rent public housing apartments. The Presleys were forced to leave their apartment for a time, but were subsequently permited to return.

"People work and they try to do the best for themselves, but sometimes it seems it just isn't worth it," Elvis once said. "There are ways you can be penalized just for being industrious and careful with your money."

When he joined Crown Electric it looked like that was the way his life was going to be forever. But fate

**107**

has a way of taking hold of a man's life and shaping it according to its own plans. In Elvis' case, fate was to play an important part in changing his life. Fate was to make him a superstar such as the world has rarely known.

There was a man named Sam Phillips in Memphis in those days, who had opened a studio at 706 Union Avenue called the Memphis Recording Service. Phillips, who had been a radio engineer and announcer in Florence, Alabama, intended the studio for "Negro artists in the South who wanted to make a record (but) just had no place to go."

Another function that the Memphis Recording Service provided was to give people an opportunity to record songs as birthday or anniversary gifts. It cost $4 in those days to cut a disk.

Sam Phillips also owned a record company called Sun Records, which he had started in 1952. Prior to that he had released his records through the Chess Label in Chicago and the Biharis West Coast RPM label.

During the summer after Elvis graduated high school he decided to make a record to give to his mother as a birthday gift. He went to the Memphis Recording Service, paid his $4, and recorded "My Happiness' and "That's When Your Heartaches Begin." Connie Francis had had a hit with "My Happiness" in the '50s, as had The Ink Spots. The song had been written in 1933, two years before Elvis was born.

Marion Keisker, who worked for Phillips at the time, was so impressed with Elvis' singing that she made a tape recording of it and insisted that her boss listen to it. Phillips was a perceptive record executive, and had been the first to record such artists as Roy Orbison, Johnny Cash and Jerry Lee Lewis. Before long he was to add Elvis Presley's name to that list—indeed, to the front end of that list!

The thing that Phillips was looking for was a white singer who could produce a black sound. In that way the music could be sold to white audiences, which was where he knew the real money was.

Elvis had visited Phillips again in January 1954 to record two other ballads. It was shortly before Elvis' 19th birthday. Phillips teamed him up with Scotty Moore, a guitarist, and Billy Black, who played string bass. The trio rehearsed until mid-June 1954.

Scotty Moore has been quoted as saying that their first record happened by accident. "It wasn't intended to be a session at all," he once recalled. "That was the reason only Bill and I were in the studio. Sam just wanted to see what would happen on tape. First thing he (Elvis) did was 'I Love You Because.' Then we did a couple of those country oriented things. Little while later we were sitting there drinking a Coke, shooting the bull, Elvis picked up his guitar, started banging on it and singing 'That's All Right Mama.' Just jumping around the studio, just acting the fool. And Bill started beating on his bass and I joined in. The door to the control room was open, and Sam come running out and said, "What in the devil are you doing?' We said, 'We don't know.' He said, 'well, find out real quick and don't lose it.' "

In that manner the rock 'n' roll era was launched. "That's All Right Mama" had been recorded over 10 years earlier by one of Elvis' musical heroes, Arthur

"Big Boy" Crudup. Elvis' crisp, clean, unaffected version differed from Crudup's more traditional blues rendition. On the flip side of the dsic, which was on the Sun label, was "Blue Moon of Kentucky," a Bill Monroe bluegrass classic.

The two songs were recorded on July 5 and 6, 1954. Now that he had cut a record Elvis was on his way to the big time—if anybody happened to buy it! Then, as today, people bought records because they heard them on the radio and happened to like them. So Phillips' most important goal was to get some airplay for the new Elvis disc. He arranged to have a tape of the records delivered to Dewey Phillips (who was no relation to Sam, by the way), a popular disc jockey at Memphis' WHBQ Radio.

Dewey Phillips hosted a program called "Red Hot and Blue," which featured rhythm & blues musci for young white listeners. He agreed to give the new disc a spin. Elvis reportedly found out that the record he had cut was going to be on the radio and couldn't bear listening to it. He went to the movies, but his parents stayed glued to their radio to hear it.

What happened is a classic example of the power of an audience. Dewey Phillips' audience loved "That's All Right Mama." They kept calling the station to demand that it be played again and again and again. They were so enthusiastic about Elvis that Phillips had a message sent to Elvis' house asking that he visit the studio as quickly as possible for an interview on the air.

Elvis wasn't anxious to be interviewed. The thought of going on the radio was kind of frightening to Elvis back in those days. But he did go over to WHBQ to talk to Phillips, who is said to have instructed him, "Shut up, sit down—and don't say anything dirty!"

Phillips was playing "That's All Right Mama," and started asking Elvis some questions about his early years and his black-sounding music. Elvis never even realized that he was being interviewed on-the-air at the time! In later years when he had new albums to promote, Elvis never made the rounds of the radio stations like most artists routinely do. He never took an active part in promoting his product at the radio stations, exchanging small talk with disc jockeys and program directors, posing for photos for the music industry trade papers and autographing pictures to be used as prizes in contests. Perhaps his lack of interest in doing radio station promotions stemmed from his frist experience in Memphis. The public may have been ready for Elvis, but was Elvis ready for the public at that point? It represented an extraordinary lifestyle change for a youngster who was then driving a truck for a living!

The next day Elvis was back at work again. But his future was not behind the wheel of a truck. Soon thereafter he plunged into his new career as a recording artist on a fulltime basis. Moore and Black were part of the Presley team in those days. They had had their own group, the Starlight Wranglers, which they disbanded so as to be able to work with Elvis.

"That's All Right Mama" was a big regional hit. It sold about 20,000 copies and even hit the Number One position on the Memphis country & western music charts. *Billboard,* the leading music industry

**111**

trade newspaper, reviewed Elvis, calling him, "a potent new chanter who can sock over a tune for either the country or the rhythm and blues markets." At the end of 1954 Elvis was honored by *Billboard* as the eighth most promising new hillbilly artist.

Elvis started appearing throughout the Memphis area at clubs like the Bel Air, the Airport Inn, the Eagle's Nest and the Overton Park Shell. He was a big local success, but was cut down to size again when in September 1954 he appeared on the "Grand Ole Opry." Reportedly, the "Opry" people told him to get his old truckdriving job back again if he could!

Things worked out much better for him with the "Louisiana Hayride" program, which made him a regular in the cast after only two guest appearances. The program was based in Shreveport, La., and Elvis' fame throughout the South began to spread. From a local success he was becoming a regional phenomenon. His back-up group was growing. In addition to Moore and Black, he had a drummer, D.J. Fontana. Their travels would take them throughout Texas and Mississippi.

Years later when Elvis would meet his untimely death, the newspapers in those southern states would fondly remember him. They would run local stories about people who remembered Elvis way back then. They would editorialize about Elvis, too. He really meant something in those states in which he had gotten his first start. To the Texans, Louisianans, Alabamans, Floridians, and Mississippians Elvis was something special. To the folks in Tennessee he was a native son.

In September 1954 Elvis cut his second Sun Record, "Good Rockin' Tonight," which hit the Number Three spot on the local country & western charts. He was known at times as the Hillbilly Cat and the King of Western Bop. The group he had formed with Moore, Black and Fontana was now called The Blue Moon Boys.

A local disc jockey named Bob Neal, who presided over an early morning radio program, entered the picture at this point as Elvis' first manager. He once recalled in an interview that Elvis "threw everything into it, trying to break that audience down, trying to get it with him. He'd always react to audience reaction, and in the rare instances where he'd be placed on the show early, I always felt he kind of outdid himself, making it tough for the next guy to follow."

Neal helped promote The Blue Moon Boys on radio, which got them engagements throughout the Southern states. They played anything from Church auditoriums to high school gyms to county fairs. Elvis' salary had shot up from $35 a week at Crown Electric to around $200 weekly. Most of his money was sent home to his parents, to whom he was always deeply devoted.

In January 1955 Elvis signed a contract giving Bob Neal the right to represent him. One of the goals Neal had was to present Elvis as something other than just another hillbilly singer. Neal thought a national television appearance on a program like Arthur Godfrey's "Talent Scouts" would be what Elvis and The Blue Moon Boys needed to hit the big time. He arranged for Elvis to get an audtion for the Godfrey program, and flew to New York with him.

But it didn't turn out well. Godfrey's casting people rejected Elvis.

Remembering Elvis in those days, Neal once told a reporter that, "He was greatly anxious for success. He talked not in terms of being a moderate success. No—his ambition and desire was to be big in movies and so forth. From the very first he had ambition to be nothing in the ordinary but to go all the way. He was impatient. He would say, "We got to figure out how to do this, we got to get ahead.' "

Getting ahead for a performer is usually a combination of talent and the right kind of management direction. In Elvis' case there was no question about his talent. As for his management, he needed someone who could figure out how to package what he had to sell and then go out and really make the big sales for him. By now it was July 1955 and Elvis had been recording for Sun for a full year. His new disc, "Baby, Let's Play House," had come out and had hit the national Country & Western charts. By the end of 1955 Elvis would be named as the most promising—not the *eighth* most promising!—artist in the country field. Of course, by that time he would be a highly commercial RCA Records artist. But that's getting ahead of our story!

During the summer of 1955 a man called Colonel Tom Parker came into Elvis' life. Parker—whose title was a strictly honorary one, but one that he has always insisted on using—had been running the Great Parker Pony Circus. He had managed artists like Eddy Arnold and Hank Snow. For Snow he had developed something known as the Hank Snow Jamboree Attractions, which turned into one of the South's most important talent booking agencies. It was through this agency that Parker and Presley first got together.

The Colonel started booking Elvis into various performing engagements throughout the South. The more he saw of the youth, the more he liked him. Also, the better Parker got to know Elvis the more ideas he had about how to turn him into a superstar. By November 1955 Bob Neal was no longer running Elvis' career management. On November 22, 1955 Col. Parker became Elvis' exclusive manager. His first major act in that capacity was to sign a deal with RCA Records by which Elvis' contract with Sun was purchased for $35,000 and another $5,000 in back royalties. Elvis got a Cadillac as a bonus for signing with RCA.

The emergence of rock 'n' roll music as an important and highly commercial type of American music was not surprising to RCA. Executives for the company saw it coming. Steve Sholes had been the head of RCA's country & western recording activities for many years. Larry Kanaga was then executive vice president of the label. Frank Folsom was another key RCA executive with an eye on the future. The three men are credited in the music industry for bringing Elvis to RCA.

Sholes is said to have said to Kanaga one day, "Larry, we must get some of those rock and rollers." Folsom reportedly had an amount of money solely for emergencies. He determined from Sholes and Kanaga that it would take $40,000 or less to bring Elvis over from Sun. He considered it enough of an emergency with regard to RCA's future to authorize spending the money.

Sam Phillips recognized a good offer when he saw

one. In those days $40,000 was a great deal of money. The recording industry had not yet reached the stage where multi-million dollar contracts were doled out on a seemingly casual basis. When Phillips finalized the sale, he is said to have told Col. Parker, "Colonel, I hope you make a million with the boy." The way things turned out, that was something of an understatement!

Looking back on the sale of Elvis' contract, Phillips once told a reporter, "I had to either sell it or give up everything I was doing and go with Elvis." He decided to continue his overall career as a record producer, and later produced such other top artists as Johnny Cash, Jerry Lee Lewis Roy Orbison and Charlie Rich.

As for Colonel Parker, he had a pretty good idea of what Elvis was all about. He had seen Elvis for the first time during a Hank Snow performance in Houston. The Colonel had been impressed with the wild audience enthusiasm for the relatively unknown Elvis and his then-new style of music. In time this led to Col. Parker taking over Elvis' management. He is said to have remarked at the time, "You stay good-looking and sexy and I'll make us as rich as rajahs." Indeed, he kept his word!

On January 10, 1956 Elvis cut his first record for RCA at its studio in Nashville. The song was known as "Heartbreak Hotel." It became Elvis' first Gold Record, having been certified by the Recording Industry Association of America as having sold at least a million copies.

Colonel Parker and RCA both knew they had been right all along. The purchase price of Elvis' Sun contract had been cheap in terms of the rewards

Parker and RCA—to say nothing of Elvis—would now reap. "When I first knew Elvis," the Colonel once noted, "he had a million dollars' worth of talent. Now he has a million dollars."

As Elvis' popularity increased so did the public criticism of his performance style. The erotic, sexual, wiggling performances that Elvis specialized in—so much so that he quickly became known as Elvis the Pelvis!—were frowned on by the ministry, by teachers and by parents.

He was criticized as being an inspiration for young hoodlums and a bad influence on teenagers. "If I thought that was true, Sir," he once said to a newspaper writer, "I would quit and go back to driving a truck. I wouldn't do anything to hurt anybody, Sir. Money doesn't mean anything to me. It's the business of singing that I love."

On another occasion, he asked his mother to comment on his stage act. "Do you think I'm vulgar in my act on stage, Moma?" he is said to have inquired.

Gladys Presley answered, "You're puttin' too much into your singin', though you're not vulgar. But keep up that kind of activity and you won't live to be thirty."

Elvis reportedly told her, "But, Moma, I just can't help it when I sing. I have to jump around. And I sure don't feel sexy when I'm singing—if that was true, I'd be in one of those institutions where they send sex maniacs."

The only place Elvis was being sent was to the top of the entertainment industry. He had made his first television network appearances on CBS-TV's Saturday night "Stage Show" series, hosted by

Tommy and Jimmy Dorsey. On January 28, 1956 it was snowing in New York, where the show was produced. Elvis, Scotty Moore and Bill Black must have shivered in the cold weather to which they were most unaccustomed. This was the big break that they had been hoping for.

Jackie Gleason was the producer of the Dorsey Brothers program. It was up against much stronger Saturday night competition from NBC-TV's "The Perry Como Show." Something had to be done to boost its ratings, and Gleason a greed to try Col. Parker's new performer. Maybe he could have some effect. Elvis was signed for six appearances, each of which brought him $1200. This was more money than he would have made driving his Crown Electric truck for four years!

When Elvis performed "Heartbreak Hotel" on the first of those Dorsey shows America sat up and took notice. As the word began to spread each week's studio audience for the program got younger and more involved in the show. Young girls everywhere were declaring their love for Elvis. He was clearly the hottest new property to come along in many years.

After his success on the Dorsey Brothers' programs, Elvis won a guest shot on Steve Allen's television show Allen's ratings climbed substantially thanks to Elvis. Ed Sullivan's "Toast of the Town" series on CBS-TV competed with Allen's NBC-TV show. The Sullivan show was watched by many more people, and represented the most important kind of exposure that a relatively new performer could get. In 1956 Elvis accepted $50,000 from Sullivan to make several appearances on his program. Some 54 million viewers were estimated to have watched Elvis perform on the Sullivan show. Although Elvis was probably Sullivan's favorite recording artist personally, Sullivan was a keen judge of public taste and recognized Elvis as a giant star.

The only thing left to do was make motion pictures. In April 1956 Elvis was given a screen test by producer Hal Wallis at the Paramount Studios in Hollywood. Wallis was best known for having produced the highly successful series of Dean Martin and Jerry Lewis comedies in the '50s.

Elvis' screen test was shot with an experienced actor named Frank Faylen. A three picture deal was the result. The first of the films was a black-and-white Civil War story for distribution by Twentieth Century-Fox called "Love Me Tender." The picture had originally been called "The Reno Brothers," but was retitled to benefit from the success of the popular Presley song from the film.

Fox released the picture just before Thanksgiving 1956. It did sensational box office business, and established Elvis as a movie star for the future. In all, Elvis starred in 33 feature films, including two documentaries about himself.

As Elvis' career ascended his whole life changed. The day came when Bill Black and Scotty Moore, with whom Elvis had been appearing onstage since the very beginning, wanted a lot more money than they were getting. Colonel Parker reportedly convinced Elvis that it was himself who was the drawing card. The fans wanted Elvis, not Black or Moore. So they were sent packing. Elvis became a single act, and that's the way he remained for the rest of his career.

Bill Black put together a new combo and recorded for Hi Records, a new label based in Memphis. When he was only 39 years old, in the fall of 1965, he died of a brain tumor. Scotty Moore left Memphis and moved to Nashville, where he became a recording engineer and a studio musician.

The one thing that threatened to hurt Elvis' career was the U.S. Army. In January 1957 Elvis was ordered to report for his medical check up. He went to Kennedy Veterans Hospital in Memphis, where he was found perfectly fit to serve. In those days, of course, service in the Army was compulsory. There was no way a public figure like Elvis could escape putting in two two years in uniform. It was rumored in 1957 that when it came time for Elvis to serve he'd get special treatment of some sort. Perhaps he'd be deferred altogether. Or maybe the Army wouldn't insist on cutting his hair to regulation soldier length. Or, perhaps, instead of doing some typical military job he'd be assigned to entertain the troops.

The standard letter asking Elvis to show up for his draft physical had arrived at his home in Memphis while Elvis was in Hollywood making his first film. The orders to report had originally come while Elvis was filming his fourth picture, "King Creole" on location in New Orleans.

Elvis had been granted a deferment on his date of enlistment to allow him to complete his work on "King Creole." Paramount Pictures could have lost some $350,000 if Elvis had had to drop out of the filming at that point. Although brief deferments of that sort were routinely granted for business purposes or to enable boys to finish their college educations, many people objected that Elvis was getting preferential treatment.

State Representative Nick Johnson from Harlan County, Kentucky resigned from his draft board, claiming that, "I cannot conscientiously ask any mountain boy to serve the country unless afforded the stame treatment as Mr. Presley."

On the other hand, many of Elvis' fans took the opposite point of view. They picketed draft boards and induction centers throughout the country insisting that the Army would be putting Elvis' life in danger. How could they dare do this to the King of rock 'n' roll?

As for Elvis, he tried as best he could to calm things down. "All I want is to be treated as a regular G.I.," he once said. "I want to do my duty and I'm mighty proud to be given the opportunity to serve my country."

There was no winning over the anti-Presley group. When they read that Elvis had been granted his deferment so as to complete "King Creole," they raised a mighty rumpus. "My boy received so such treatment," one mother complained. "It's indecent that you should let this monster Presely make the entire Army do as he wants."

On March 24, 1958 Elvis was inducted into the Army. His parents accompanied him to the Memphis draft board, where Colonel Parker was also on hand to supervise a going-away press conference.

Elvis was asked if he had any fears about tough treatment in the Army. What about the rough sergeants he might run into? He said that if he did get a rough time, "it won't be because of anything I do to provoke it. I'm going in to be a soldier and the Army can do anything it wants with me and send me any place."

Elvis also told reporters, "I have a duty to do and I'm gonna do it." The Governor of Tennessee sent him a message that noted, "You have shown that you are an American citizen first, a Tennessee volunteer, and a young man willing to serve his country when called upon to do so."

By contrast, another message was received from a fan who insisted, "Release Elvis Presley immediately. It's unfair—you didn't put Beethoven into the Army."

It was an unusual day for Elvis. He had started out early that morning as an important Hollywood movie star and a major recording artist. By day's end he was merely Private Presley, US Army number 53310761. The induction ceremony had been unlike anything the Memphis draft board had ever witnessed before. A jammed press conference complete with balloons promoting Elvis' next feature film, "King Creole."

As for Elvis, he was dispatched to Fort Chaffee in Arkansas. There one of the first things that happened to him was that the camp barber cut off most of his hair. Colonel Parker is said to have remarked at the time, "I know a lot of people that would pay a lot of money for that hair." They never had the opportunity, since it was burned along with the hair of many other newly-arrived recruits.

There were stories in the newspapers about how Elvis' paycheck was being cut to about $80 a month. What the papers didn't report was that Elvis would still be drawing at least $1,000 weekly thanks to his royalties from records, music publishing rights, merchandising and movies. The big loser, of course, was the Internal Revenue Service. With Elvis' earning power virtually stopped, he had somewhere close to $500,000 less to pay in income taxes now!

When Elvis arrived at Fort Chaffee he received $7 cash, which was given to each recruit for spending money until their first payday. A reporter asked him what he was going to do with the $7, and Elvis joked, "Probably start a loan company." The way things turned out, he had to spend $.65 of it to pay for his required haircut.

But Elvis turned out to be a good recruit. He got through basic training so well that his colonel told the press, "I never expected this. He turned out to be an honest and forthright young man. My impression of what he was certainly changed as soon as he came here. He had to put up with a lot of things, in terms of publicity and ribbing from his mates, and most of us would have found it hard to take. But he's leaving us with a good wholesome feeling."

While Elvis was in the Army it was up to Colonel Parker to keep the public from forgetting him. In 1957 Elvis had worked particularly hard to stockpile recordings for future release, and to complete the movie "King Creole." RCA issued his LPs and singles on a regular basis now that he was in the service. They also started releasing LP collections of his "gold" records, which sold very well. When "King Creole" was released in July 1958 Elvis started getting some good reviews for his acting ability.

In August 1958 fate took a hand in Elvis' life once

again, but this time in a tragic sense. Elvis' mother, Gladys, became ill. At this point Elvis was stationed at Fort Hood in Texas, where he had rented a four room house in the nearby town of Kileen. His parents stayed there, along with various Elvis friends who might drop in, and enjoyed being close to Elvis' Army base.

Elvis' plan had been to leave shortly after basic training for service in Germany. He was planning to take his entourage of family and pals along with him. What he hadn't expected, of course, was that his mother would suddenly be taken ill. Gladys Presley was a strong woman, who had worked very hard all her life. But in July 1958 she changed dramatically. She no longer had her customary energy. The spark of life was no longer there.

When this change in Mrs. Presley became apparent, her husband took her home to Memphis to see the doctor. His diagnosis was hepatitis. Elvis was granted emergency leave and flew home to be at her beside. Elvis was very devoted to his mother. He remained at her bedside for some 36 hours without sleep. Finally, at midnight on August 14, 1958, just as the new day was getting underway, his father told him to go home and get some rest. Three hours later Vernon Presly had the sad duty of calling his son to tell him that Gladys had died of a heart attack.

Elvis was distraught. He rushed back to the hospital and threw himself across his dead mother's bed. He sobbed uncontrollably. There were many reporters present, but Elvis was unable to talk to them. The loss was a particularly difficult one for him to bear. The loss of a beloved mother is always a tragedy for a son who has been deeply attached to her.

Elvis reportedly wanted to hold his mother's funeral at Graceland, his Memphis mansion. He had always looked on the house as being a memorial to his mother, and he felt it was an appropriate place for her funeral "because Momma loved my fans and they have the right to say a last farewell to her."

But the final decision was not to hold the service at Graceland. Instead, Gladys Presley was laid to rest at Forest Hill Cemetery in Memphis. She was 46 years old.

At Gladys Presley's funeral some 3,000 people, mainly from Tennessee, showed up. There were about 400 invited mourners. There was a dignified service, which included a gospel group called The Blackwood Brothers. They sang "Rock of Ages," one of Mrs. Presley's favorite hymns.

Elvis had a huge monument erected in honor of his mother in the Forest Hill Cemetery. The inscription on her tombstone noted that, "SHE WAS THE SUNSHINE OF OUR HOME." When Elvis was in Memphis he would find time to visit the cemetery and pay his respects to his late mother.

On one occasion Elvis had said of his mother that she had the strength of a salmon fighting its way upstream, the soft looks of a doe, and that she was a loving mother. Her dedication to Elvis had been extreme, possibly a result of his twin brother, Jesse Garon, having died at birth. Elvis' having been spared meant all the more to her in view of that initial tragedy.

One of Gladys Presley's last requests had been that, should anything happen to her, Elvis and Vernon should continue to remain close. Now, with her passing, Elvis was returning to the Army and was to be sent to Germany. His unit was to make up a replacement there in the Third Armored Division, which was General Patton's old outfit. Plans were quickly put together for Vernon to accompany his son to Germany. Elvis was respectful of his mother's wishes and he and his father stuck together until death took Elvis away.

Elvis sailed for Germany on September 19, 1958. His troop ship left from the Military Ocean Terminal in Brooklyn, New York. For the embarkation Colonel Parker arranged the same sort of press attention that he had put together for Elvis' induction into the Army. The Army brass at Fort Hood was happy to see him go. Not that he hadn't been a good soldier while there, but the 15,000-odd fan letters addressed to Elvis each week were putting a terrible strain on the local postal system!

Naturally, the press wanted Elvis to talk about his mother's passing. He explained, "Apart from being a real friend, she was my advisor. She'd always try to slow me up if ever I thought I wanted to get married. She was right—it helped my career not to get married."

Little did Elvis know that he was sailing in the direction at that very moment. Now that his mother was no longer here to help and advise him, he was going to meet a girl who would convince him to give up bachelorhood.

As for his career, it was booming in spite of his disappearance from the scene. Elvis captured the Number Four spot on the charts at the end of 1958 with "One Night." He started 1959 with the big hit, "A Fool Such As I," and that summer topped the music charts with "A Big Hunk O'Love." His LPs also continued to sell well. The papers were always running stories about how Elvis had turned into quite an accomplished soldier in Germany. He was gone but certainly not forgotten.

In Germany Elvis was quite famous, too. When his troop ship, the General Randall, sailed into the harbor at Bremerhaven there were some 1,000 screaming German fans to greet Elvis. It was a rousing reception by German standards, although in the United States it would probably have been ten times greater.

While Elvis was stationed in Germany he drew close to 10,000 fan letters each week. Somehow they all found their way to him, even those addressed only to Elvis, U.S. Army. The military establishment knew exactly where Elvis was! There also were a great many phone calls, some of them from across the ocean, from Elvis fans who wanted to check up on how he was getting along. It wasn't easy for the Army to cope with having Elvis Presley in its ranks.

Although the Army granted no special treatment to Elvis, he was permitted to live off the base. His father and grandfather had flown over, and had rented a home for the remainder of Elvis' stay in the Army. So every morning Elvis was driven in his limousine from his posh home to his Army camp. There he was busy working with tanks. It was a far cry from the life he had come to know over the last two years.

In spite of it all, Elvis continued to be the good soldier. One commanding officer pointed out in an interview, "He's fooled us all. We had our stomach full to here of these celebrities, singers and actos, and we figured Presley for just another lightweight. But he's never angled himself into anything easy and he shows exceptionally good judgement for a kid worth a few million dollars. This guy Elvis has made it popular to be a good soldier. It's great for us."

Indeed, there was even talk about the possibility of Elvis re-enlisting. Colonel Parker reportedly had a make-believe newspaper front page printed up with the banner headline "ELVIS TO RE-ENLIST." The page was supposedly stuffed with a regular newspaper and delivered to Hal Wallis, producer of Elvis' early films. It's a wonder Wallis didn't keel over from shock on reading the phony newspaper!

Announcement had already been made of Elvis' first movie project out of uniform. It was called "G.I. Blues," and put him back in khaki once more. Obviusly, Elvis' fans wanted an opportunity to see what they had been missing. They wanted to see how Elvis performed as a soldier, and Hollywood was determined to let them to buy tickets to find out for themselves.

Just as Elvis' singing and acting career had progressed well, his military career did, too. Late in his service Elvis was given the responsbility of commanding a three-man reconnaissance team in the 32nd Scout Platoon.

On March 5, 1960 Elvis completed his service in the Army and was released. He was a free man again. He was ready to resume the career that he had left behind two years earlier. He was free to grow his sideburns back once again!

If there had ever been any doubts about just how popular Elvis would be once he returned to civilian life, they were immediately dispensed with. Elvis cut a single called "Stuck on You," which rapidly rose to the top position on the music charts. It proved beyond the shadow of a doubt that there still was an enormously dedicated market for Elvis' music.

Another question that must have been on Colonel Parker's mind at the time was would there also be a market for a married Elvis? If there wasn't, not only would Elvis suffer but so would the Colonel. Reportedly, the arrangement between the two gave Parker a minimum of 25 per cent of every dollar Elvis earned. Some reports speculate that 25 percent is a very low figure, and that the Colonel's take is substantially greater. In any event, it's clear that he's earned every dollar thanks to his brilliant management of Elvis' career.

Marriage was in the offing. Elvis had met a young lady named Priscilla Beaulieu during his last months in Germany. Something clicked when he first laid eyes on this dark-haired beauty. She was very young when they first met. Priscilla was not even a 15 year old schoolgirl in 1960. Her father was an Air Force captain, who was later to be promoted to the rank of colonel. Priscilla was going to high school in Wiesbaden, Germany at the time.

She was a beautiful girl even then at an age when many girls are still gawky teenagers. Priscilla had already blossomed. Her eyes were grey and her hair was dark red, although in black-and-white newspaper photos it always looks black.

Elvis once told an interviewer that Priscilla, "was just a kid—more than ten years younger than me, but she wasn't like so many of the other girls. I guess most of 'em were a little overawed by me, but what

I'm supposed to be. Dunno why, because I'm shy myself and do my best to make other people feel at ease. But with this check it was different. She didn't give the impression she was in any way tongue-tied."

With Elvis' departure for America the romance with Priscilla might never have happened. But Elvis was determined not to lose track of this beautiful and intriguing young girl. He called her father and won his permission for Priscilla to visit Elvis for Christmas 1960. He had to find out for himself if he was truly in love or if it was a mere infatuation. When he realized it was love Elvis arranged with Priscilla's father for her to return to the U.S. and live in the Presley home. He gave all necessary assurances that he would be most respectful of her, and that they would marry at the right time.

Elvis put Priscilla through school in Memphis, provided her with cars—first a Corvair and then a lavender Chevy sports coupe—and plenty of spending money. On May 1, 1967, when Priscilla was 21 and Elvis was 32, they were married in Las Vegas. The story was the top news of the hour, and the lead report in the newspapers of the time. Elvis had personally picked up the $15 marriage license from the Clark County registrar.

Some 100 invited guests joined the Presleys for a wedding breakfast after the simple ten minute ceremony—which omitted the traditional word "obey" from the vows—was completed. Salmon, oysters, fried chicken and an endless supply of champagne composed the menu. Priscilla's favorite, "Love Me Tender," was played in her honor.

In an interview Elvis had been asked how it felt to be a married man. He replied, "Priscilla is something really special. There have been, in the past, girls I have liked better than other girls, but I never before fell completely in love with any one girl. But I've always looked basically for qualities of love and sincerity and trust. There was a girl, when I was starting out as a singer. Maybe she didn't take me seriously, but as soon as I started touring, she upped and married another guy. That broke my heart...In fact, it made me wary of ever being so hurt again. I felt for that girl the way my father felt for my mother when they first met. I know that to be true, because I talked to my dad about it."

After their wedding, Elvis and Priscilla slipped off for a four day honeymoon. There wasn't time for anything longer since Elvis was hard at work filming "Speedway." Production on the picture had started in June. The following month Elvis was proudly announcing the fact that he was going to become a father. As he put it, "We really hadn't planned for one this early, but it seems to me that this is what marriage is all about."

On February 1, 1968, precisely nine months to the day that Elvis and Priscilla were married, Lisa Marie was a great joy for Elvis, and his new position as a family-man is said to have resulted in a new excitement on his part about re-conquering the music industry and Hollywood. His drive for sucess became greater than ever before.

As is so frequently the case with Hollywood marriages, the necessary separations that result from location filming put a great strain on the bonds of husband and wife. Elvis was around only infrequently. Priscilla had plenty of money, but very little to do. She became bored.

Another negative force on their marriage was the presence of Elvis' group of old buddies, nicknamed the Memphis Mafia. These old friends of his from the early and poor days of his youth were paid to be with him at all times. They helped cheer him up, played football with him, ran errands, and helped with any number of necessary chores that were now unfit for Elvis to do for himself.

Priscilla and the Memphis Mafia had to wind up as enemies. They both were dependent on Elvis, and they both craved his time, love and affecion. Elvis spoke about the Memphis Mafia in any number of interviews. "They are all members of the Corporation of which I am the head," he once pointed out. "But even if they work for me, they are still all my friends."

On another occasion he pointed out that, "My boys are nearly all about my own age. They don't earn a fortune, but they do collect enough. We never have any fights about money. Most of them are from Memphis. We have the same roots, the same blood, the same emotions, the same heritage and traditions and I find it a great comfort to have people around me who are like precious pieces of furniture from my own boyhood home."

Priscilla was up against some pretty formidable competition. It's worth noting, this competition had had Elvis all to themselves for a great many years. Priscilla reportedly once referred to them as "goons who stick to Elvis like so many burrs." There could be no compromise between the two forces. One would have to go.

In 1973 Priscilla and Elvis were divorced. She had apparently tired of living in what some have described as "a gilded cage." All the money in the world just wasn't sufficient to keep her there. In February 1973 she left Elvis for Mike Stone. her karate instructor. She wanted to return to the normal world. Being Mrs. Elvis Presley had put a strain on her that she could no longer endure.

Reportedly, her divorce settlement with Elvis brought her over $1.5 million and alimony of more than $7,000 a month, plus a surprise gift of 5 per cent of Elvis' record royalties. She was once quoted as saying that, "We really hardly saw each other and when we did there were all his other pals around. Things did change a lot when Lisa arrived, but they changed back again when he left our home in Hollywood to work in Las Vegas."

Elvis' conquest of Las Vegas began in 1969, when the old International Hotel—now the Las Vegas Hilton—opened its doors. Thirteen years earlier Elvis had played Vegas, but had failed. In 1956 his appeal was strictly to the younger generation. The type of people who frequented Las Vegas then tended to be older and more conservative. In recent years Vegas, too, has changed and is now attracting a somewhat younger crowd. But when Elvis made his Vegas debut there was little enthusiasm for him.

By 1969, however, things had changed. Elvis was the second act to play the International—the hotel had opened with an appearance by Barbra Streisand—and he proved to be a dynamite act. It had been 13 years since he had worked live onstage and he was more than a little nervous about his "comeback."

Elvis played the International for a month. His fee came to more than $500,000, according to newspaper reports. His shows ran an hour a piece, and were filled with about 20 songs. "That's All Right Mama," which had started everything going for Elvis, was one of them. Backing Elvis onstage was a group of three black girls; the Sweet Inspirations.

At a news conference at the time Elvis told reporters, "I'm really glad to be back in front of a live audience. I don't think I've ever been more excited than I was tonight."

His comeback had obviously been a smash. The audience had loved him. They couldn't get enough of him. Elvis continued, "Sometimes when I walk into a room at home and see all those gold records hanging around the walls, I think they must belong to another person. Not me I just can't believe that it's me."

From 1969 on Elvis became a major Las Vegas act. He always played the International and quickly became one of that hotel's key acts. Elvis' shows would all be sold out months in advance. You had to know someone to get in without having planned it far ahead.

When Elvis was appearing at the International the hotel helped to promte his act in ways that were unusual even for Vegas. All the hotel staff would wear buttons and hats honoring Elvis. There were plenty of Elvis banners, signs and posters advertising his live appearance in the International's showroom. His tapes, albums and photos were sold in the hotel. It was clear that the International was Elvis' hotel!

"When he appeared in '69 and '70, doing four-week engagements, two shows nightly, he drew more than 100,000 in a room which accomodated,

2,000," Bruce Banke, publicity and advertising director for the Vegas Hilton, said in an interview after Elvis' death.

"Whenever Elvis came to town it was like a major city-wide convention. Just being here drew thousands of people who did not necessarily go to the shows. Fans came from all over the world to see him. We would have groups booked in from Europe and Japan that would bring in 50 people, taking 50 rooms and booking reservations for every show."

Elvis played the International from 1969 through 1975, appearing twice a year. In 1976 he did only one engagement, from December 1-12. There had been tentative plans for Elvis to appear at the Hilton's brand new sports entertainment pavilion in the Fall of 1977.

Elvis and Vegas were an ideal pair. They were well suited for each other. Vegas is an all-night town, and nobody thinks twice if you want to have breakfast a 4 p.m. or dinner at 6 a.m. People sleep when they want to. Some don't sleep at all. Anything goes in Vegas. If there is a sense of morality there it's not anything like most people are used to back home. For Elvis, Vegas was a shot in the arm. He drained the energy and vitality that his audiences provided and this, in turn, revitalized him. Vegas made him feel young and alive. It brought out the very best in him as a performer, and it gave him an immediate highly-charged emotional response from people who loved him.

Vegas is a superstar town. Elvis was the epitome of the superstar of our time. He grew into the role in a way that no one could have predicted back in 1955. From an arrogant looking punk kid, who could sing and wiggle in a way that nobody else could then, Elvis developed into a more mature entertainer with terrific stage presence.

He never forgot his roots. In his later years the wiggle was still there when he sang, but he had learned how to get a laugh from it. On one occasion he reportedly asked his Vegas audience, "There, see that movement?—they wanted to send me to prison for that!" It was funny because it pointed up how times had changed. In 1955 that kind of wiggling drew charges from clergymen that Elvis was immoral and a corrupting influence on teenagers. In the moral climate of the 1970s, Elvis' wiggles were relatively pure and innocent. They weren't very corrupt in comparison to the porno movies that were sweeping the nation.

Unlike a great many performers who did well in the '50s but failed to develop and grow as the times changed, Elvis managed to bridge the gap. To do so he devoted his life to his art. There were casualities, including his marriage.

Some who knew him maintain that Priscilla was the only person Elvis ever loved, other than his mother. Some said he loved Priscilla because she seemed to him to be very much like his mother was. Even after Elvis and Priscilla were divorced he refused to speak badly of her, and even refused to allow anyone else to badname her. He took her departure with karate chopper Mike Stone very badly. There have been reports alleging that Elvis wanted to have Stone killed. But this is something that will never really be known. Those who are inclined to believe it will; others will have their doubts.

On one occasion before his marriage Elvis remarked that, "Any girl in my life would find it hard because she'd have to live up to the standards of my Mom. The proudest day of my life was when I gave her a pink Cadillac. It was a silly sort of thing. But she and I knew what it meant—that all the bad years were over. That Cadillac is still parked in Graceland. It's a sort of memorial to her."

The closeness that Elvis felt for his mother was unique. He is said to have never felt the same way about his father, although they stayed together after Gladys' death. Elvis always took very good care of his father, and left him most of his estate.

Vernon Presley had met Davada Stanley—who was known as Dee—while Elvis was stationed in Germany. Dee was married at the time to Sergeant Bill Stanley. An attractive blond in her 30's then, she had three children, Billy Jr., David and Ricky. After a short time, Bill and Dee were divorced, leaving her free to marry Vernon.

Elvis never denounced the marriage, but there have been reports since that it displeased him very much. He is said to have commented that if it made his father happy it was fine with him. But the question raised was did he really believe that or was he unable to bring himself to give voice to his true feelings?

In any event, On November 15, 1977 it was reported that Davade had obtained a Dominican Republic divorce from Vernon Presley after seventeen years of marriage.

The relationship between Elvis and Vernon and Dee was outwardly a good one. In fact, when Elvis convinced Priscilla's father to allow her to return to the United States years before they would marry, he arranged for her to live with Vernon and Dee in their home near Graceland. It provided a respectable residence for Priscilla, but kept her readily accessable when Elvis wanted to see her.

By August 1977 Priscilla was long gone. His mother was long gone. His freedom to come and go in any normal fashion was also long gone. When Elvis wanted to see a movie he couldn't go downtown and buy a ticket. He had to rent a movie theatre. Sometimes he rented amusement parks so as to be able to enjoy himself in the ways he used to like before fame and fortune caught up with him. About the only thing Elvis had left were his old buddies, the Memphis Mafia, that the Colonel had originally assembled to keep Elvis' spirits high. And in Elvis' later years, discussed elsewhere in this book, the Memphis Mafia reportedly was keeping more than just his spirits high!

With his death the final chapter of the Elvis Presley Story ended. The filing of his will in which nothing was left to Priscilla is said to have surprised her friends. Since Priscilla had split with Mike Stone in 1976 she and Elvis had remained close. There were even reports that he had been trying to call her on the night he died. Reportedly, Priscilla wasn't in when Elvis called, and when she phoned back she was told that Elvis was asleep. Since she didn't want to disturb him, she said she'd call again tomorrow. But tomorrow never came for Elvis.

One theory is that Elvis was calling to tell Priscilla that he and Ginger were going to be married. But an old girlfriend of Elvis', Linda Thompson, has challenged that theory. She told a reporter that although Ginger has been telling the press that she and Elvis would wed, "He didn't tell any of us he had such plans—and I'm sure he would have if that was what he had intended."

She also pointed out, "I didn't know anything about it. Neither did Priscilla or his father—and we all feel that it wasn't Elvis' style. He only knew her a few months. He and I lived together for five yeas, until we decided to go our separate ways earlier this year."

Whatever the truth, no one will ever know now. And, in any event, with Elvis dead it would hardly seem to matter. In the period immediately after his death there were a number of developments. On August 26, 1977 it was reported that the William Morris Agency, which had represented Elvis for over 20 years, would now handle both Vernon Presley and Col. Tom Parker. Included in that representation would be exclusive rights for film and television versions of Elvis' life story.

As for Elvis' fans, they continued to hold onto their tickets for what would have been his final concert tour. About $600,000 worth of tickets was outstanding. The theatres holding that money were asked to donate it to charities. But before that can be done the theatres need to have the tickets back, or at least some portion of them, for accounting purposes. The fans don't want their tickets mutilated since that would lessen their souvenir value.

There was no easy solution to the problem. In New York, where Elvis was to have performed at the Nassau Coliseum on Long Island, all funds from unreturned tickets were placed in an interest-bearing bank account. Elvis' fans were given until 1983 to make their refund claims. What happens in 1983 if not all the money is claimed? Whoever is the state's comptroller at that point will have to wrestle with the problem.

Looking back on Elvis' life, Sam Phillips, without whom there most likely would never have been anything but a truck-driving Elvis, commented, "You know, I think it's entirely possible to die from a broken heart. I think that was a contributing factor. This man needed to be allowed to do what he wanted to do. Let him be seen on the streets. It may have taken a few guards at first. But I feel as fervently as I feel anything that he would be alive today if that had happened."

Phillips also recalled how, "when he had signed for his first appearance in Las Vegas, he called me. He said, 'Mr. Phillips, I just go to have you come out. I'm scared to death. I got to have somebody I know, some friend, in the audience.' "

In Phillips' opinion, "It's a vicious cycle. You start out and you're so proud of your success and you say, 'God, I'll do anything to stay on top.' And when you find yourself saying, 'I know it's going to be over before too long and I've got to keep up this image. I'm mortal, but I can't let people know I'm mortal.' But there's just no such thing as being an island unto yourself."

Frank Sinatra, appearing at the Alpine Valley Music Theatre in Wisconsin, told his audience that with Elvis' death he had lost a "dear friend and a tremendous asset to the business."

Chet Atkins, Vice President of RCA in Nashville, who knew Elvis from his very early days, reflected that, "When he came along, he was so different in everything that he did. And I think that was one of the big reasons he had such great impact on the business. He was the first to start the thing about rhythm. He dressed differently and moved differently from anybody we had ever seen. He was electrifying. I don't think anything like this will ever happen again, at least not in my lifetime. And I don't think there will ever be another like him."

Ray Walker, a member of The Jordanaires, Elvis' long-time back-up group, said he wasn't surprised. "This wasn't really sudden. Elvis had been in bad health for the past two or three years. In fact, more seriously than he knew himself."

There were tributes from the three principal music industry newspapers. *Billboard* observed that, "Presley's legacy—like that of other great musical stylists—remains in the grooves of his recordings. And they will be around forever." The paper also noted that, "He started out as a rebel and ended up a legend."

*Record World* wrote that "Elvis was the one figure who more than anyone else singlehandedly reshaped and redefined the perimeters of the music industry during its formative years—at once becoming its most controversial figure and ultimately its most successful and influential rallying point."

*Cash Box* called him "the American Dream personified—from his humble beginning through his rise to fame...Elvis—a consummate person and performer. He lent an air of dignity that elevated the entire profession of entertainment. Always polite and gracious, Elvis maintained a sense of class that distinguished him from his fellow entertainers."

The old Memphis Recording Studios at 706 Union Avenue were being talked about as a possible official Memphis landmark to honor Elvis' memory. Jud Phillips Jr., nephew of Sam Phillips and now an executive for Phonogram/Mercury Records, told reporters that, "A number of organizations have looked into the situation, but, for whatever reason, nothing has been done. This has been discussed a number of times (prior to Elvis' death) and each time it comes up and interest rises, the price goes up. The people who are currently holding the property are totally unaware of the aesthetic value. They are looking at it only as a piece of property, capital."

Perhaps President Jimmy Carter, a Southern boy himself who could easily understand what Elvis was all about, said it best. In a brief memorial statement about the King's passing, the President explained, "His death deprives our country of a part of itself."

The President also said that Elvis "was unique and irreplaceable. More than 20 years ago he burst upon the scene with an impact that was unprecedented and will probably never be equal-led."

And so the life that began on January 8, 1935 in a two-room shack ended on August 16, 1977 in an 18 room mansion. The king was dead. And, for once, there was no new King to speak of.

# CHAPTER SIX

## THE DARK SIDE OF ELVIS

*"Frankly, we're all pretty shaken up by
the erratic way he's been behaving lately,"
a friend of Elvis confided.*

In the period immediately before Elvis Presley's death it was evident that something terrible was happening to him. There were reports that Elvis was hooked on drugs, that he was close to having a nervous breakdown, that he was impossible to get along with, that he was grossly overweight, and that he was living in a state of total unreality.

There is no way of knowing for certain what the truth was. Only Elvis could have set the record straight, and he is not giving interviews. But it is possible to construct from various sources a frightening picture of the American dream gone sour. The image one sees is that of the local boy who made good getting so carried away with his new life of luxury that he just couldn't handle it.

The poor boy who thought driving a truck was going to be his ultimate station in life was suddenly thrust into superstardom at the age of 20. Nothing in his background had prepared him for fame and fortune. He had had no training to be an international idol, nor had he had much education to speak of. His ability to sing was unquestioned. But what about his ability to survive in the rarified atmosphere of Hollywood and Las Vegas?

Show busness is a rough profession. From the outside it looks like a bed of roses. The money is fantastic, the girls are beautiful and available, and the fans are generous with their love. What could be better?

In reality, of course, show business is something else. It's the kind of business that eats people up alive. It burns them out at very young ages. When show business is through with you the chances are nobody else will ever want you. Just as quickly as show business creates its heroes, it destroys them. Today's star is tomorrow's nobody. The slogan of the entertainment world is, "Don't call us, we'll call you." Of course, they never do!

Elvis was unique in that he rode the show business lion for over 20 years. Nobody manages to stay in the saddle that long. But Elvis did. But it took a tremendous toll from him. Could it have been avoided? Was there anything Elvis could have done to outsmart the fates? Could he have resisted the temptations to indulge and, worse yet, to overindulge?

Again, there are no easy answers. It's easy to say that nobody forced him to overeat, to abuse his body, to lose his respect for those who served him with great loyalty and affection. But under the circumstances of his new life at the top it's easy to see how something like that could have happened. It's more than possible to understand how Elvis could have drifted into what we can call The Dark Years, without ever once realizing what was happening to him.

That may well be the key to the entire situation. If he had seen and comprehended how he was changing for the worse he might have been able to stop in time. He could have reversed his decline and fall. But he never saw it coming, and nobody ever had the perception, the desire or frankly, the guts to tip him off.

One of Elvis' closest friends confided to a reporter—under a cloak of anonymity—that he King of rock 'n' roll was acting like a true King in his later years. "Frankly, we're all pretty shaken up by the erratic way he's been behaving lately," he explained. "Everyone is alarmed—and we're worried because he doesn't seem to be getting any better."

What was wrong? For one thing, Elvis had become hot-tempered in his daily dealings with people. He was increasingly more difficult to get along with, they have said. His nerves were frequently on edge, and he required constant pampering. One of the ways in which his nervous condition manifested itself was in his eating habits.

Like so many other red-blooded American boys, Elvis was devoted to what might best be called "junk foods." These are the hamburgers made from everything but beef, the greasy fried chickens, the soda pops, the pizzas dripping with high calorie and high carbohydrate ingredients, etc. We all know what they are because we all enjoy eating them.

Dr. George Nichopoulos, Elvis' personal physician, had ordered him to go on a strict diet. But Elvis wasn't the kind of patient that a doctor can intimidate. You couldn't push Elvis around, not even if you had a degree from medical school. It just didn't work that way. Elvis was the boss. He did what he chose to do. If dieting didn't happen to fall into that category, there wouldn't be any dieting. It was all pretty cut and dried.

Elvis had weighed about 175 pounds when he was in good condition. By the time he died his weight was over 200. Some reports even put it as high as 230 pounds. The weight was altogether evident in his bloated face and in the folds of fat hanging over his belt.

On one occasion Dr. Nichopoulos was quoted as saying that, "Junk food has plenty of nutrition in it. It's just that Elvis eats so much of it. It is like some people who drink too much beer. They don't have the discipline to stop. Elvis is human, like anyone else. He sometimes finds it a little hard to keep up the discipline. Right now he is on a diet and he is going to be in great shape."

But that prediction never came true. Elvis never got back into what anyone could objectively call "great shape." At least not on a long time basis. Once he is said to have dropped about 60 pounds of bloat from his frame. But it didn't stay off for long. And as we all know, it goes back on so much quicker than it comes off!

A business associate of Elvis told a reporter that, "His weight must be back in the 230's and he wears it all out in front. He split his pants on stage not long ago and he's very uptight about that. Now he keeps the gyrations down while he's performing."

One psychologist put it this say: "Like any other man his age, Elvis tends towards depression. The weight problem is bad for his self-image, although many of his fans might not care. It's bad for Elvis because it changes his own mental attitude. He is probably unsure of his sex appeal, which would be made worse by the fact that he almost certainly equates sex appeal with success."

It recalls Colonel Parker's comment to Elvis many years ago about how if Elvis stayed "good-looking and sexy," the Colonel would make them "both rich as rajahs." The wealth poured in, true to his promise. But what would have happened in the years to come with Elvis looking the way he now did?

From the accounts that have been made public, being fat was only one of Elvis' problems, and not the most important problem at that. Ever since his Army days Elvis has been fascinated with guns. He was probably very happy during his basic training when he had the opportunity to fire an M-1 rifle and other firearms. Over the years Elvis reportedly built up a sizable collection of guns and police badges. While the badges aren't very dangerous, the guns are.

On one occasion, according to an anonymous

source who talked to a newspaper reporter, Elvis nearly killed Ginger Alden, his fiancee. This source has been quoted as saying, "She had threatened to leave him, and Elvis chased after her with his gun, fired a shot over her head and told her: 'You come back into this house.' Then he returned to the house—and so did she. It was Ginger's actions that caused Elvis to shoot over her head. From the way it's been described to me, she's running him ragged. She is playing games with him."

The allegations continued: "Ginger is repeatedly telling him 'no,' when he's used to having his every whim obeyed and that's driving him crazy. For the first time in his life somebody is telling him no. Ginger still won't do what she's told. For example, she doesn't like Nashville and when Elvis was due to go there for a recording session, she wouldn't go. There was a big argument about it and Elvis threw a tantrum. He went to Nashville alone—but he wouldn't record. He spent three nights in Nashville while the musicians sat cooling their heels. Finally, he flew back to Memphis to be with Ginger. Elvis then rescheduled the recording session at is personal studio at Graceland. But he didn't like the sound he'd produced on the recording. So he told everyone to stand back, pulled his gun and blasted away into the speakers."

Reports of this type of violent activity by Elvis are not new. For instance, a girl who knew Elvis reported once that she had been terrified by the fact that he shot out the television set screen in his Las Vegas hotel suite in her presence. He reportedly told her not to worry about it because the hotel knew to just put it on his bill!

Elvis' attitude seemed to be that thanks to his money he was able to come and go as he pleased. He was allowed to do things that others couldn't do becuse they couldn't afford the consequences. But he seems to have never understood that there were more than monetary consequences to his actions in many instances.

On January 8, 1975 Elvis was 40 years old. It was a depressing age for him to have attained, and his health wasn't good. That very same month he entered Baptist Hospital in Memphis. The press was told that he was there because of severe fatigue and a twisted colon. But there were many rumors to the contrary.

Some people thought he had liver trouble, possibly the same hepatitis that had brought about his mother's death. Others thought there could be some drug difficulties. No one really knew except his doctors, and they never went beyond the official statement to the news media.

In March 1975 Elvis was back in action, and appeared before sell-out crowds at the Las Vegas Hilton. He quipped, "You should have seen me a month ago. I looked like Mama Cass!" He even confessed that he had still another 20 pounds to shed before he could feel comfortable performing. A crash diet was usually his method. We don't know if he used diet pills at all or, if he did, in what quantities.

One of Colonel Parker's associates, Tom Diskin, was quoted at the time with reference to various rumors about Elvis. "I hear these rumors about this and that in Elvis' private life," he said. "I just pay no heed. He's entitled to live his own life the way he wants and it's not for his management figures to try to interfere."

The rumors continued even after his death. One of the most fascinating was the one heard in Nashville and Memphis that Elvis had been suffering from cancer. Supposedly it was the cobalt treatments he was secretly receiving that caused him to gain so much weight.

It was also remored that Elvis had buried himself in the Bible upon learning that he had a terminal disease. In the past there had been other reports about his religious interests. One of his associates told a reporter that Elvis "has Bible readings all the time." Another suggested that Elvis "believes that God put him on earth as a special person to bring a lot of happiness to a lot of people. One day we were in front of the mansion when Elvis said, 'Did you notice they cleared the skies for my birthday?' He really believed the skies were cleared for his birthday!"

Others have told eerie stories about Elvis' devotion to his long dead mother. Since her funeral in 1958 Elvis had reportedly kept her bedroom at Graceland locked. It has been reported that when she died a pane of glass in her window was broken. The story goes that Elvis has never had that broken pane repaired. Everything remains just as it was while Gladys was alive.

One of the spookiest stories about Elvis has got to be the following, attributed to one of Elvis' friends. He states that Elvis has heard his mother's voice! "All the guys there [at Graceland] have heard it," he said. "They were all sitting around the dinner table one night when a woman's voice was heard calling his name. Elvis looked at all the guys around him and they looked at him. Then a couple of guys stayed around Elvis with their guns drawn and the rest of them went through the house with their guns out—but they couldn't find anyone. When he went to bed, Elvis again heard the voice—coming from his mother's room. So he does believe he's in contact with his mother."

If you believe in the supernatural you may accept that story. But most people will probably have considerable trouble in doing so. But even those who are sceptical will have seen the magazine stories in the months before Elvis' death, and will have had some thoughts put into their heads by headlines such as: "ELVIS ON VERGE OF NERVOUS BREAKDOWN!" or "HAS ELVIS LOST HIS SNAP, CRACKLE & POP?"

Perhaps the most consistent rumor about Elvis was that he was hooked on drugs. After his death an autopsy was performed, and the Shelby County, Tenn. medical examiner, Dr. Jerry Francisco, issued a report. His findings surprised many people. "There was no evidence of any abnormal, illegal drug use," he revealed.

Dr. Francisco did note that, "I can't say he was taking no drugs at all because his own doctor has said he was taking appetitie depressants." Most of us would probably call such drugs "diet pills."

Continuing his report, the doctor also pointed out that he had not found any needle marks on Elvis' body. There would have been a number of visible needle marks if he had been taking any drugs that were injected with hypodermics. He also said there was no sign of any damage to Elvis' organs or body tissues, which might have been the result of heavy drug use.

As for pills, Dr. Francisco's report was that had Elvis been popping them in the quantities alleged by some people there would have been visible evidence on examination of the body.

In effect, Elvis got a clean bill of health from the medical examiner. Newspapers across the country carried the story. A typical headline was that from the Omaha *World-Herald* of August 18, 1977: "DOCTOR: NO EVIDENCE OF DRUGABUSE."

A principal source of the rumors about Elvis is the book, "Elvis: What Happened?" by Red West, Sonny West and Dave Hebler as told to Steve Dunleavy. The book is a fascinating, gripping account of what Ballantine Books calls on its front cover, "The dark other side of the brightest star in the world!"

The Wests and Hebler were Elvis' bodyguards and insist that they were the only people in a position to really know what was going on in the King's private life. Red West, 41, had been a childhood friend of Elvis' and on at least one occasion when they were both in high school saved Elvis from being beaten up because some older kids didn't like his ducktail haircut. Sonny West, 38, is Red's cousin, and served as an Elvis bodyguard for 14 years. Dave Hebler, 38 is a karate instructor, and was a bodyguard for Elvis since 1974.

The bodyguards' book is a highly controversial expose of what may or may not have been the real Elvis. Some of the charges that are alleged in it make fascinating reading.

Elvis is said to have gotten into the habit of taking pills—uppers and downers—while he was stationed in the Army in Germany. Drugs and liquor had never been anything that Elvis had bothered with before that. To the end of his days alcohol held little interest for him, but the pills are said to have entered his life for good during his years in Germany.

Another interest stemming from his German period is said to have been his devotion to karate. That too, was something he picked up on in the Army.

Just as Elvis had reportedly gotten his first dexedrine pills from an Army sergeant, the bodyguards charge that it was Elvis who forced them to pop pills. Elvis wanted his bodyguards to be able to keep up with his own frantic non-stop schedule.

There are a number of stories in the book that point up Elvis' grim determination to get whatever he wanted. In one case he set his heart on obtaining for his collection of police badges a Federal Narcotics Bureau badge. He attempted to get one through the proper channels, but reportedly was turned down by Deputy Narcotics Bureau Director John Finlator. All he could issue Elvis, Finlator explained, was an honorary badge. But that wouldn't satisfy Elvis. He wanted the real thing!

He ultimately got one, too. But it took a personal meeting in the Oval Office of the White House with then-President Nixon to bring it about. Elvis had no qualms about using his status as a superstar to get what he wanted.

Sometimes what he wanted was alive. The bodyguards stated that Elvis had bragged about never having had to pay to get a girl. But when Priscilla ran off, they wrote, Elvis had a constant need to have girls around. They charge that on various occasions they arranged for several hookers to be brought to his hotel suite because it delighted Elvis to watch them make love to one another. For a price these girls would satisfy what the bodyguards claim was Elvis' taste.

Another story in the book presents Elvis' cruel streak. He is said to have had a habit of introducing one of his featured singers, Kathy Westmoreland, in a manner that suggested she was sexually promiscuous. This is said to have not been the case, and Miss Westmoreland was troubled by the fact that she was starting to get obscene phone calls from people who believed Elvis' introductions. She asked Elvis' road manager, Joe Esposito, if he could ask Elvis to introduce her in some other way. Reportedly, he did this in a very diplomatic manner.

The effect, however, was humiliating for Kathy and for the back-up group, the Sweet Inspirations. Elvis made reference to the fact that Kathy hadn't liked his previous introductions of her, and then said she could "get the hell off the stage-- if she didn't approve! This was in Greensboro, North Carolina before a packed house. Both Kathy and two of the Sweet Inspirations did depart, leaving Elvis to perform before a highly embarrassed audience.

Having worked for Elvis for so many years, there is no end to the number of stories about him that the bodyguards maintain are true. They write that during one holiday to Vail, Colorado in January 1975 Elvis was presented with a surprise birthday cake by his then-girlfriend, Linda Thompson. None of the bodyguards knew she was going to surprise Elvis with the cake, so none of them were on hand for the ceremony. Afterwards, they claim, Elvis chewed them out for having missed the big moment!

During the same trip then-President Ford's daughter, Susan, was in town. There was going to be a party in her honor and she asked if Elvis would attend. He reportedly turned her down, but agreed to see her if she cared to visit his chalet. A King is, after all, more important than the daughter of a mere President!

The bodyguards also write about Elvis' marital troubles. They present in detail the events involving Priscilla's leaving Elvis for her karate instructor, Mike Stone. Elvis had first met Stone in Hawaii when he and Priscilla were there on their brief honeymoon in 1967. He saw Stone again in January 1972 during an Elvis performance at the Las Vegas Hilton. Elvis introduced both of them, and later they came back to his dressing room.

The bodyguards say that Elvis, a karate expert himself, had wanted Priscilla to learn the art, too. As a result of their conversation it wound up that Priscilla started taking karate lessons from Stone about three weeks later.

Before long, write the bodyguards, a romance had blossomed between Stone and Priscilla. Details began to come out, and some of them were brought to Elvis' attention. The bodyguards give Priscilla a lot of credit for having refused to cheat on Elvis, as they say she easily could have done for a long period. They applaud her decision, which they call courageous, to tell Elvis she was leaving him. And they indicate understanding of her situation because of Elvis' lack of attention to her.

In a highly effective conclusion to the story, they maintain that Priscilla did not tell Elvis for whom she was leaving him and he actually didn't know. He is said to have broken the news to the bodyguards, complaining that he had given Priscilla plenty of freedom to have her own life. Indeed, he told them, he had even encouraged her to take karate lessons because she was interested in the sport. It was then that the bodyguards revealed to Elvis that it was Mike Stone, himself, who had won Priscilla's heart!

The bodyguards' story is quick and fascinating reading. They insist that it is the whole truth, and it may very well be. But we can't say for absolute certain. Only Elvis, himsef, could have refuted it. Shortly before his death there were reports that Elvis was very upset by the book's contents. He was said to have been angry and bitter about his former buddies having treated him in this fashion. If he had lived, it's entirely possible that he might have brought a law suit against them. Perhaps he would have ripped their book apart, giving his side of the story. As things stand, it is a one-sided report. Those interested in pursuing the subject will have to read it and try to come up with their own conclusions.

Elvis' life was as close to being the American Dream come to life as possible. He was dirt poor at first, and filthy rich at the end. He started out wanting to be somebody, and he wound up having become *something*. The person, Elvis, had long ceased to exist. In its place was the thing, Elvis Presley/Superstar.

What killed Elvis? The doctors say his heart stopped. Within a matter of four minutes time he was dead. No amount of help would have saved him, they insist.

When he died he was living a life somewhat similar to that lived by Howard Hughes. Shut up in well-guarded retreats, protected by bodyguards night and day, attended to by loyal men, not eating well, and possibly abusing their bodies with drugs, both Presley and Hughes saw their lives end. While Hughes was the mystery man of his day, Elvis was someone we all thought we knew. No one saw Howard Hughes. But Elvis Presley was always around. You could see his movies, buy his record albums, and in the old days occasionlly view him on television. You could catch his shows in Las Vegas. It was up to you. Elvis was there for the asking—really, for the *buying*.

But was he really there, after all? Apparently not. The Elvis we knew—thought we knew is probably a better way of putting it—wasn't the real Elvis. Oh, no.

And who was the real Elvis? Well, he may have been that small boy at the beginning of *Citizen Kane*. You remember—the boy who had nothing at the time but his sled, and was playing so happily in the snow drifts. The boy who grew up to become rich and successful, who owned the world, so to speak. The boy who wound up with everything. The boy who wound up with nothing.

Somewhere in the early morning hours of August 16, 1977 that little boy closed his eyes and, at last, went to sleep.

# CHAPTER SEVEN

## REMEMBERING ELVIS—ABC'S SKLAR

*"Without Elvis Presley you could
not possibly have had the Beatles,"
Rick Sklar explained.*

The rise of Elvis Presley was closely tied to the birth of contemporary radio throughout the United States. Before Elvis broke on the scene in the mid-'50s radio stations didn't sound anything like they do today. The music they played, of course, was very different, too. There were no rock 'n' roll radio stations since there was no rock 'n' roll yet! The music of the 1950s was sweet and syrupy until Elvis arrived. Then things started to change.

Rick Sklar is now Vice President of Programming for ABC Radio. When Elvis first happened Rick was a programming executive for New York radio station WINS. Although there were several stations that joined WINS in picking up on new rock 'n' roll music that appealed to the teens, WINS was particularly good at packaging those brand new sounds. The station became the leader in the country's most important radi market, and had a tremendous influence both on the music business and on the sound of modern radio.

Alan Freed, who coined the phrase "Rock 'n' Roll while working on Cleveland radio, was on the disc jockety staff at WINS when Elvis first appeared. Freed had been the pioneer DJ in the playing of black music—rhythm & blues, as it was known—for white audiences. When Elvis started releasing records, Freed was ready to spin the new sounds for his growing radio audience.

In the years after Elvis arrived on the scene, Rick Sklar left WINS and joined WABC Radio (New York) as its program director. Thanks to Rick the station soared to the top of the New York ratings, where it still is today. Interestingly WINS dropped rock 'n' roll years ago, and is not an all-news station.

An expert on Elvis Presley and anything having to do with rock 'n' roll music, Rick was interviewed on WABC—TV (New York) on the evening news immediately after Elvis' death. He agreed to talk about Elvis in an exclusive interview for this book, for which the author is most appreciative.

Our conversation about Elvis went as follows:

MAG: When Elvis Presley first happened in 1956 where were you, Rick?

RS:     At WINS Radio in New York.

MAG:    If memory serves, WINS was a pioneer rock 'n' roll radio station.

RS:     That's right.

MAG:    Before Elvis, what kind of music was the station playing? And how did it change when he came in?

RS:     That's a very good way to begin. In 1955, the last year before Elvis Presley broke on the scene, the Number One song on the station for the year as "Cherry Pink and Apple Blossom White" by Perez Prado. Other big songs that year were Mitch Miller's "The Yellow Rose of Texas," "Autumn Leaves" by Roger Miller, and The Four Aces were singing "Love Is A Many Splendored Thing." You might also remember The McGuire Sisters' "Sincerely." Now those were the biggest songs of the year. The only hint of what was to come—the one song that they played that year that was not like those others—was Bill Haley and The Comets' "Rock Around the Clock." That gave us a hint of what was to come. The next year Elvis Presley broke on the scene.

MAG:    When you say Elvis broke on the scene, was that when he was already at RCA Records or was he still recording for Sun Records in Memphis?

RS:     Well, the first we heard of him at WINS, I think he was already at RCA. When he came to our attention it was with a really big song.

MAG: Did RCA know what they had at the time?

RS: They would have had to because that year three of the Top Ten songs were by Elvis Presley—including the Number One and the Number Two songs of the year! He hit with "Heartbreak Hotel," which went to Number One. "Don't be Cruel" was Number Two song of the year. "Hound Dog" was Number Six. And wedged in between those songs was still the older type of music. Like Nelson Riddle's "Lisbon Antigua," "My Prayer" by The Platters, and Gogi Grant's "The Wayward Wind."

MAG: When you started to play Elvis' music, what kind of reaction did you get from the WINS listeners?"

RS: They loved it. They bought everything they heard. We also played that year—Elvis had the Number 14 song, "I Want You, I Need You, I Love You," and the Number 15 song, "Love Me Tender." As you can see, he was a pretty big part of the cast of characters that made up the musical artists on the station that year.

MAG: How did the disc jockeys at the station react to him? Was Alan Freed at WINS at that time?

RS: Yes. Alan Freed had been playing what he had called rock 'n' roll music. He made up that term—he and Bob Smith—to describe the rhythm & blues music that they were playing at that time, which essentially was black music played to white audiences that had never heard the stuff before.

MAG: Did you get any feeling of polarization of, say, teenagers and their parents then? Were parents in 1956 anti-Elvis?

RS: Well, this was a complete break with that other music that the parents did accept. You did get a very definite polarization. This was rock: Presley was the synthesis of country, rock and the black rhythm & blues or soul music. And he brought it altogether, and he became the expression of American rock 'n' roll. This was to form the foundation for popular American music in the years to come. So now when we look back, rock is now the root of American popular music.

MAG: When Elvis broke and began ejoying this success were there a lot of imitations that followed quickly?

RS: It took a while. Much of the material even in the next year—we go ahead one year to 1957, Elvis was all over the charts again. The Number One song and the Number Two songs were, again, Elvis Presley. "All Shook Up" and "Jailhouse Rock." You still had The Four Lads singing "Standing On The Corner," and you had "Moonglow and Theme From Picnic." But mixed in with it was Bill Haley and The Comets doing "See You Later, Alligator." And "Blueberry Hill" by Fats Domino. But you still had domination in that year by Pat Boone with his "I'll Be Home." Vic Damone was still big. The Platters were very big. Bing Crosby was still singing. He had "True Love" that year with Grace Kelly. Little Richard was coming along with rock music like "Long Tall Sally." So it was a mixture at that time.

MAG: You mentioned Fats Domino and Little Richard, both of whom are, of course, black artists. Now prior to Elvis, am I right in thinking that the black recording artists were not getting airplay on stations that were oriented to white audiences?

RS: That's correct. Prior to Elvis, and prior to Alan Freed. That's how Freed made his name.

MAG: Is it fair to say that the success of Elvis helped open the door to more exposure for black artists?

RS: Sure, because the acceptance grew for that sound.

MAG: Let me come back to 1956 for a minute. When Elvis happened was there a reason? Were the times right for something to happen then? It was the middle of the Eisenhower Years when, allegedly, nothing happened at all! What would you think of Elvis' timing?

RS: His timing was perfect because many artists can release material, but it is only when the public goes for it that you know that the timing was right. For him to hit the Number One and Two songs of the year in his first year, in a sea of sweet, syrupy music, you can see that the youth that buy the records instantly responded. It touched a chord. It was something that they needed. It fullfilled a need.

MAG: Do you see a big difference between the kids of 1956 and the kids today, 21 years later, in terms of their musical tastes and what they will accept?

RS: The kids of '56 were the first ones to accept rock. The kids of today accept it. They were just born into it. This is their music. There's a lot of softer rock that they will accept now. Presley, of course, was more sexual in his music. He was more blatant and open about things that were sung in a quiet, softer way by others.

MAG: Did the sex appeal that he projected have a lot to do, do you think, with his success?

RS: Yes, I think so. Definitely.

MAG: I recall that when he was on The Ed Sullivan Show they would only show him from the waist up.

RS: Yes, in those days it was scandalous to show him moving his hips.

MAG: Did he ever come around to the radio stations and do any promotion of his records in person in those early years?

RS: No. He was very different in that regard from any other artist. His manager—Col. Tom Parker, kept him at a great distance. I think that, personally, he was reticent to mix too much in the industry, and he didn't. He never did.

MAG: Yet he had that astounding success just the same.

RS: Oh, sure. He was carried by his talent, not by any hypoing. And by smart management.

MAG: How did the radio station handle Elvis at the time? Were there contests involving him on WINS?

RS: No involving Elvis. There was airplay of his records. Basically, it was airplay.

MAG: In other words. it was not the way it was years later when The Beatles came over. There was a tremendous amount of exposure of them on the air and look-alike contests, etc.

RS: By then rock was so established that we had a different atmosphere and could do that. Here the music itself, the impact, was so different that the music carried it.

MAG: The impact of the music was, of course, not only on the teens who bought it, but also on the future musicians of the world. What kind of impact did Elvis music have on the future of rock music?

RS: Well, he made it. He gave it to *all* of America. It had just been specialized until then. And he built the foundations on which others could follow.

MAG: The Beatles have said that they were influenced by him.

RS: Without Elvis Presley you could not possibly have had The Beatles. I think that John Lennon ackowledges this. He frequently wears this large diamond pin on his lapel. It's a large pin, and it's all diamonds. And it says, "ELVIS." I think he's acknowledging there the foundation that Elvis built.

MAG: Most of Elvis' songs didn't seem to be about anything too important, the way music is today. Would you comment on that?

RS: They were talking about relationships between the sexes, mostly. Love songs have always been the key ingredient of music. It's in the way he expressed it.

MAG: When he started to make motion pictures, which was not too long after his records started coming out, did this have an even greater effect on his popularity?

RS: It kept him up there certainly. But the records and the concerts were the mainstays. Movies had a reinforcing effect certainly. I think the records helped the pictures as much as the pictures helped the records.

MAG: So it was a good combination?

RS: Oh, yes.

MAG: In terms of Elvis over the years, what happened to him? He went through a period in the 1960s from which many artists wouldn't have recovered at all.

RS: Ironically, what happened to Elvis Presley was The Beatles. he was swept aside by The English Invasion because every year until 1964 he was on the Top 100 Charts, and he was selling records and we were playing them. The first year that we weren't was 1964, the year of "She Loves You" and "I Want To Hold Your Hand." The year of The Beatles, Gerry and The Pacemakers, The Dave Clark Five, The Animals. He was literally swept aside by The British Invasion.

MAG: Of course, radio was sounding a lot different by then. Your music mix no longer had some of the sounds of the mid and late '50s, did it?

RS: Radio had become more specialized. Top 100 had given way to Top 40, which was beginning to give way to Top 30. The playlists on the radio stations were shrinking. The audiences were becoming more demanding.

MAG: So the times had changed. The English wave had swept Elvis out. And yet he came back from all that!

RS: Eventually, he came back. In 1964 he was swept off the charts. In 1965 he did get a song in the Top 100—"Crying In The Chapel." And then nothing happened until 1969, when he had "In The Ghetto" and "Suspicious Minds." Then in 1972 he had "The Wonder Of You" and "Mama Liked Roses," which was one record. It didn't do that well, but it did okay. It came in as Number 72 for the year. Then he had one more, "Burning Love," in 1972 that was really big.

MAG: Do you think that he was affected or changed by this sudden drop from being at the very peak of his popularity?

RS: I'm sure. It would affect anybody. Certainly.

MAG: Yet he came back in 1969 when he opened in Las Vegas at the International Hotel. Suddenly, he had a whole new career as a major entertainer.

RS: Frank Sinatra had a second career. Tony Orlando, as you remember, had two careers, too. So have others.

MAG: A lesser performer, a person of less stature, might have just been crushed by it and disappeared. What qualities did Elvis possess, do you think, that accunted for his ability to come back?

RS: First of all, he had real talent: it wasn't hyping or other people's arrangements. He had the essential ability to deliver material and to deliver it in a unique way that was acceptable to a great many segments of the

American public. When he made his come-back he was working on the old generation plus another generation that was coming along. It was 15 years later. So we're now into two generations.

MAG: The adults who originally hated him and said that he was a bad influence on their kids and so forth, did they ever come around? Or was it that the kids grew up and became adults themselves?

RS: I think the kids grew up. some of the adults, the younger ones, eventually grew to accept him through the mass media, television appearances, motion pictures and the continual bombardment of the songs everywhere on the radio. A new generation of kids heard and liked some of his stuff. The other kids who had been with him in '56 were growing up. So you had three groups there.

MAG: The overall management and direction of his career that Col. Parker took care from almost the very beginning when it started to happen, has been cited by some people as superintelligent, and very smart. Others have criticized it and said that the strategy may not have been the best in the world. What do you think of the management of Elvis' career?

RS: I think it was superb. I don't know how you could have improved it.

MAG: One of the criticisms sometimes encountered is that Elvis, as a film star, made so many movies that were insignificant, unimportant, and trivial. Today people seem so much more selective about the films that they do. He did, in fact, 32 movies over the period from 1956 to '70. There was a final film, a documentary, in 1972. That makes 32 pictures altogether.

RS: I'm sure the movies all made money because his public was not going to the movies to see great works of art. They were going to see Elvis, and they were going for escapism and to be entertained. I suppose there were two different ways you could do it. You could do a block-buster film every three or four years—maybe every two or three years—or you could do 33 films and hit them that way. I think that either way would work. I'm sure commerically they accomplished their objective.

MAG: The process by which someone becmes a superstar, is it different today than it was in 1956? Is it harder today?

RS: Some of them have to work for a long time. They don't seem to just burst on the scene anymore. This year's top of the chart artists, Peter Frampton and Fleetwood Mac, had a rough time getting up there. Fleetwood Mac was at it for ten years! Frampton did not click initially. In fact, even Elton John didn't click initially the way Presley did. He didn't just burst on the scene. They worked at it for a while. Elton John, first in England and then over here.

MAG: Elvis just happened. In a fireball. Bang! He was there one day.

RS: Right. He became part of the American psyche. He became part of people's lives.

MAG: In terms of that kind of success happening, if he came along today and sang as he had been in recent years with the kind of material he had done in, say, the last five or ten years, do you think that Elvis Presley, the newcomer of 1971 or '72, would have been successful?

RS: I think a lot of it would have been lost. He would have been moderately successful. But a lot of it would have been lost because there wasn't the contrast with what else was happening. He was an innovator in his time.

MAG: There's been talk in recent years of his having gotten into the drug scene, and being on the verge of a nervous breakdown, or being distraught over different matters. I can't ask you if there's any truth to that. But were those rumors in general circulation in the music business?

RS: From time to time you would hear something. But in the music business you hear rumors about everybody. It's a rumor type of business. And you tend to discount them after a while.

MAG: What was he like in person? Had you seen him at a concert?

RS: Yes, I saw in in New York at Madison Square Garden. I thought it was one of the best produced, most professional concerts I've ever seen.

MAG: What kind of reaction was there from the audience?

RS: Oh, they loved it. Now this was in the revival period. It wasn't that many years ago. You had mostly an audience that had been teenagers in 1956, '57 and '58. But you also had a lot of young kids along with them, and they loved it.

MAG: Was there a difference between the way audiences reacted to Elvis and the way they reacted to The Beatles?

RS: I don't think you can compare The Beatles phenomenon with anything else. It's just not fair to do that. There's a completely different type of situation. When The Beatles appeared there was mass hysteria to such a degree that there was no time during the concert when you could hear the concert. The screaming from the audience was continual. From the moment The Beatles appeared until they disappeared, all you heard was the audience screaming. For someone who never went to a Beatles concert that may seem odd to imagine. But that is precisely what happened. It happened at their first appearance in America at

Carnegie Hall in New York, at which I was present, and at both Shea Stadium concerts in New York, at which I was also present, at the Hollywood Bowl and everywhere else they appeared.

MAG: Were audiences more inclined to listen to Elvis?

RS: You had hysteria for a few minutes, but then they quieted down and listened to him sing.

MAG: Did Elvis' music reflect the times in which he was living? Did he lead his audience into new thoughts and, perhaps, actions? Or did he follow them and reflect what they were already doing?

RS: I think he touched an existing emotion in them. He gave voice to what they, the youngsters, were feeling. He wasn't really leading them. But he was a voice, a spokesman, in his singing and in his method of presentation, his movements, to what was within them. So he performed the way they felt, and they flocked to him.

MAG: But he didn't try to move them, as for example some artists today seem to do.

RS: No, he wasn't leading them. He was exactly where they, the youth, were. The older generation may have thought this was leading because they didn't understand it at all.

MAG: Did he grow as an artist in the sense that, for

example, The Beach Boys did? They started out doing songs about how nice it was to live in the California Sunshine and to play in the surf. Then, as the years went by, they started doing songs about how we were polluting the rivers and so forth. They began to express some social concerns.

RS: Certainly Elvis eventually adapted to social concerns with a song like "In The Ghetto." But, generally, he was as big the first year when he broke artistically. He came out full blossom—and he stayed there.

MAG: What happened when the news about Elvis' death frist broke in New York City?

RS: He was just about to appear at a concert here. It came as a complete shock, totally unexpected. It really was. In fact, almost everyone going to the concert hung onto their tickets and refused to turn them in to get their money back.

MAG: Was that because they didn't believe that he was really dead?

RS: Oh, no. They believed it. But they were trying to hang on to a part of him. He was an integral part of so many people. A part of America was gone. The tangible part of him that they still had were the tickets. So they held them. Few turned their tickets in!

MAG: It's an interesting phenomenon. The impact of his death across the country was front page, banner line news. Top of the page stories, photos, spreads inside the papers. In view of how little he had been doing in recent years, it was something of a surprise to see this kind of tribute to him.

RS: I think he was still an important selling catalog artist for RCA, probably one of their biggest. The span of time in which he hadn't hit at the radio station head covered a long period. So the very new listeners, the youngest ones, coming along are into other things. His impact had spread over so many years and so many people, and regionally, of course, in the South, in particular, he was so strong, that the coverage of his death is not really that surprising to me. And, remember, he died relatively young, too.

MAG: I noticed some interviews with the managers of record stores across the country in the music trade papers this week. Many of them were saying the same thing—'You know, before he died, we had his records in stock. They sold. But there wasn't such a tremendous demand for them.'

RS: Now they have $30 million week!

MAG: Suddenly, everybody wants an Elvis Presley record collection. Tell me, how do you follow an act like this? Can you?

RS: You mean, will someone else come along?

MAG: Yes. Is there another Elvis-to-be somewhere out there now?

RS: Someday, somewhere, there will be. But

they're very rare. They don't come every day. They don't come every year. They don't even come every generation.

MAG: Is there anybody today whose success and popularity approaches what Elvis had?

RS: No, because no one at the moment is making a clear break with everything that exists and coming in with something new that is touching that responsive chord.

MAG: Someone once said that there is a combination of ingredients that is vital for success as a superstar—The person has to have exposure on television, exposure in motion pictures, and exposure in records. Without any one of those ingredients the success can't approach the maximum. In Elvis' case, he had all of that going for him.

RS: When you say records, I take it you mean radio?

MAG: Yes, because records that don't get played on the radio generally don't get sold.

RS: You've got to reach the people, and you can't do it all with concerts. Today we live in a media age, and people communicate electronically. So you've got to have radio, television and then there's motion pictures.

MAG: What do you think of the sudden boom in Elvis memorabilia like banners, bumper stickers, T-shirts, magazines and, even books like this one?

RS: Again we're back to people wanting some tangible part of the Presley legend to stay with them.

MAG: As for his ultimate end. Is this a case of show business having burned out another performer and isolated him from doing anything approaching normalcy?

RS: I don't know if that's really true to that extent. Doctors and life insurance actuaries will tell you that it's possible to genetically predict the life span of a person because there's an inherited factor there. If you check back, Elvis' mother died in her forties. So you have this sort of factor in his life. So this could have happened to him if he was an insurance agent instead of a recording artist.

MAG: Or even if he had kept driving that truck for Crown Electric!

RS: We'll never know.

# CHAPTER EIGHT

## AN ELVIS DISCOGRAPHY

*"If I could find a white man who had the Negro sound and the Negro feel, I would make a billion dollars," Sam Phillips promised.*

It all happened because Elvis loved his mother. His entire career as a singer might never have become a reality if he hadn't decided to record a song back in 1953 to give to his mother as a birthday present. He was working as a truck driver for the Crown Electric Company in Memphis at the time, making about $35 a week. The $4 that it cost him to record the gift for Gladys Presley represented a lot of money to him in those days.

The songs he recorded were "My Happiness" and

"That's When Your Heartaches Begin." The work was done at the Phillips Recording Studio in Memphis, which had been opened a year before by Sam Phillips.

Phillips, who had been graduated from Auburn University with a degree in audio engineering, had recently started a record company. He called it Sun Records. He was looking for a particular type of sound, black music sung by a white artist. As he put it at the time, "If I could find a white man who had the Negro sound and the Negro feel, I could make a billion dollars!"

When Phillips heard Elvis cut his birthday gift record he felt the youngster had potential. He invited him to do some recording experimenting at Sun, and teamed him up with two sidemen, Bill Black, who played the bass fiddle, and Scotty Moore, a guitarist.

A couple of months went by without anything remarkable happening. But one day everything just seemed to click. Elvis was playing a $12.95 guitar that his father had given him several years earlier. He started singing "That's All Right, Mama" between takes, and Black and Moore joined in. Phillips knew right away that this was the black sound/white artist combination he had been looking for.

On July 6, 1954 Phillips released Elvis' first commercial record. It featured "That's All Right, Mama" on one side, and "Blue Moon of Kentucky" on the flip side. It did very well on a regional basis.

On the heels of that success, Sun Records released four other singles by Elvis. These included: "Good Rockin' Tonight" and "I Don't Care If The Sun

Don't Shine"; "Milkcow Blues Boogie" and "You're a Heartbreaker"; "Baby Let's Play House" and "I'm Left, You're Right, She's Gone"; and "Mystery Train" and "Forget To Remember To Forget."

At the same time, Elvis started going on the road with Black and Moore, and playing in nightclubs throughout the South. Things started to go well for him, and RCA Records decided Elvis was worth signing. RCA's Steve Sholes contacted Phillips and arranged to buy Elvis' contract from Sun Records. The deal was closed in return for about $35,000 in cash and a Cadillac. It was the first of many Cadillacs that Elvis would own in his lifetime. Indeed, on many occasions later in his life he handed out Cadillacs like gumdrops to perfect strangers to whom he took a liking! Elvis' funeral procession, too, was led by a fleet of 11 white Cadillacs.

It was television that helped launch Elvis on a national scale. Many people recall his appearances with Ed Sullivan, and think that they were Elvis' debut on the home screen. But that isn't the case. Elvis was brought to TV by the unlikely combination of Tommy and Jimmy Dorsey!

The Dorsey's had a summer replacement program on the CBS Television Network back in the mid-1950s. It was called *State Show,* the first of which took place on January 28, 1956.

On the initial program, where he sang "Blue Suede Shoes," Elvis reportedly met with little audience enthusiasm. No one really knew much about him, and the adults in the audience didn't know what to make of his music. They applauded when the studio applause signs were turned on. Over the course of the following six weeks, teenagers found out about Elvis and started turning the show on. Moreover, teens started joining the studio audience. By the sixth show that Elvis appeared on, there was genuine applause for his singing. By then "Heartbreak Hotel" was already well on its way to becoming Elvis' first gold single.

By the time Ed Sullivan introduced Elvis to his CBS-TV audience of some 54 million viewers on his Sunday night "Toast of the Town" series, Elvis was already a big star. It was now 1956, and the rock 'n' roll era had been born. Elvis was already so controversial that the Sullivan program refused to show him on camera below the waist! The gyrations had to be left to the audience's imagination, but they knew what was going on. Before too long, they would be clamoring for much more of Elvis.

During the period of 1956-77 Elvis had 82 singles released that sold a million or more units, making them Gold Records as certified by the Recording Industry Association of America. In order of their release they were:

(1) "Heartbreak Hotel"
(2) "I Was The One"
(3) "I Want You, I Need You, I Love You"
(4) "Hound Dog"
(5) "Don't Be Cruel"
(6) "Love Me Tender"
(7) "Any Way You Want Me (That's How I Will Be)"
(8) "Too Much"
(9) "Playing For Keeps"
(10) "All Shook Up"
(11) "That's When Your Heartaches Begin"
(12) "Loving You"

(13) "(Let Me Be Your) Teddy Bear"
(14) "Jailhouse Rock"
(15) "Treat Me Nice"
(16) "Don't"
(17) "I Beg Of You"
(18) "Wear My Ring Around Your Neck"
(19) "Hard Headed Woman"
(20) "I Got Stung"
(21) "It's Now Or Never"
(22) "A Mess Of Blues"
(23) "Are You Lonesome Tonight?"
(24) "I Gotta Know"
(25) "Can't Help Falling In Love"
(26) "Rock-A-Hula Baby"
(27) "Return to Sender"
(28) "Where Do You Come From?"
(29) "Anything That's Part Of You"
(30) "Good Luck Charm"
(31) "She's Not You"
(32) "(You're The) Devil In Disguise"
(33) "Bossa Nova Baby"
(34) "A Big Hunk O'Love"
(35) "Stuck On You"
(36) "Little Sister"
(37) "Surrender"
(38) "Ain't That Loving You Baby"
(39) "Viva Las Vegas"
(40) "I Feel So Bad"
(41) "Kissin' Cousins"
(42) "One Broken Heart For Sale"
(43) "A Fool Such As I"
(44) "Wooden Heart"
(45) "Crying In The Chapel"
(46) "Blue Christmas"

(47) "Frankie and Johnnie"
(48) "Love Letters"
(49) "Spinout"
(50) "The Big Boss Man"
(51) "Guitar Man"
(52) "Stay Away"
(53) "We Call On Him"
(54) "Let Yourself Go"
(55) "Almost In Love"
(56) "Charro"
(57) "His Hand In Mine"
(58) "Clean Up Your Own Backyard"
(59) "Mama Like The Roses"
(60) "Puppet On A String"
(61) "If I Can Dream"
(62) "Kentucky Rain"
(63) "In The Ghetto"
(64) "Don't Cry Daddy"
(65) "Suspicious Minds"
(66) "The Wonder Of You"
(67) "I've Loved You"
(68) "Patch It Up"
(69) "I Really Don't Want To Know"
(70) "Where Did They Go, Lord"
(71) "If Every Day Was Like Christmas"
(72) "Only Believe"
(73) "I'm Leaving"
(74) "It's Only Love"
(75) "An American Trilogy"
(76) "Burnin' Love"
(77) "Raised on Rock"
(78) "Take Good Care Of Her"
(79) "Separate Ways"
(80) "T-R-O-U-B-L-E"

(81) "It's Midnight"
(82) "My Boy"

Elvis issued a total of 66 record albums, all of them on RCA, during the period 1956-77. The LPs follow, along with the year that each was released and its RCA catalog number:

(1) "Elvis Presley" - 1956 - LSP 1254
(2) "Elvis" - 1956 -LSP 1382
(3) "Loving You" - 1957 - LSP 1515
(4) "Elvis' Christmas Album" - 1957 - LSP 1035
(5) "Elvis' Golden Records" - 1958 - LSP 1707
(6) "King Creole" - 1958 - LSP 1707
(7) "For LP Fans Only" - 1959 - LSP 1990
(8) "A Date With Elvis" - 1959 - LSP 2011
(9) "50,000,000 Elvis Fans Can't Be Wrong - Elvis' Gold Records, Volume 2" - 1959 - LSP 2075
(10) "Elvis is Back!" - 1960 - LSP 2231
(11) "G.I. Blues" - 1960 - LSP 2256
(12) "His Hand in Mine" - 1960 - LSP 2328
(13) "Something For Everybody" - 1961 - LSP 2370
(14) "Blue Hawaii" - 1961 - LSP 2426
(15) "Pot Luck" - 1962 - LSP 2523
(16) "Girls! Girls! Girls!" - 1962 - LSP 2621
(17) "It Happened At The World's Fair" - 1963 - LSP 2697
(18) "Fun In Acapulco" - 1963 - LSP 2766
(19) "Elvis' Golden Records, Volume 3" - 1963 - LSP 2765
(20) "Kissin' Cousins" - 1964 - LSP 2894
(21) "Roustabout" - 1964 - LSP 2999
(22) "Girl Happy" - 1965 - LSP 3338

(23) "Elvis For Everyone" - 1966 - LSP 3450

(24) "Harem Scarum" - 1965 - LSP 3468

(25) "Frankie & Johnny" - 1966 - LSP 3553

(26) "Paradise, Hawaiian Style" - 1966 - LSP 3643

(27) "Spinout" - 1966 - LSP 3702

(28) "How Great Thou Art" - 1967 - LSP 3758

(29) "Double Trouble" - 1967 - LSP 3787

(30) "Clambake" - 1967 - LSP 3893

(31) "Elvis Sings Flaming Star and Others" 1968 - LSP 3921

(32) "Elvis' Gold Records, Volume 4" - 1968 - LSP 3921

(33) "Speedway" - 1968 - LSP 3989

(34) "Elvis-TV Special" - 1968 - LSP 4088

(35) "Elvis Sings Flaming Star and Others" - 1969 - CAS 2304

(36) "From Elvis In Memphis" - 1969 - LSP 4155

(37) "From Memphis To Vegas/From Vegas To Memphis" - 1969 LSP 6020
To Memphis" - 1969 - LSP 6020

(38) "On Stage (February, 1970)" - 1970 - LSP 4362

(39) "Elvis In Person At The International Hotel, Las Vegas, Nevada" - 1970 - LSP 4428

(40) "Elvis Back In Memphis" - 1970 - LSP 4429

(41) "Elvis —That's The Way It Is" - 1970 - LSP 4445

(42) "Elvis' Worldwide 50 Gold Award Hits, Volume 1, Numbers 1,2,3 and 4" - 1970 - LPM 6401

(43) "Elvis Country" (Also known as "I'm 10,000 Years Old") - 1971 - LSP 4460

(44) "Love Letters From Elvis" - 1971 - LSP 4579

(45) "Elvis Sings The Wonderful World of Christmas" - 1971 - LSP 4579

(46) "Elvis—The Other Sides-Worldwide Gold Award Hits, Volume 2, Numbers 1,2,3, and 4" - 1971 - LPM 6402

(47) "Elvis Now" - 1972 - LSP 4671

(48) "He Touched Me" - 1972 - LSP 4690

(49) "Elvis As Recorded Live At Madison Square Garden" - 1972 - LSP 4776

(50) "Fool" - 1973 - APL 1-0283

(51) "Elvis, Volume 1 - A Legendary Performer" - 1973 - CPL 1-0341

(52) "Raised On Rock" - 1973 - APL 1-0388

(53) "Elvis - Aloha From Hawaii Via Satellite" - 1973 - VPSX 6089

(54) "Good Times" - 1974 - CPL 1-0475

(55) "Having Fun With Elvis On Stage" - 1974 - CPM 1-0818

(56) "Elvis As Recorded Live On Stage In Memphis" - 1974 - CPL 1-0606

(57) "Promised Land" - 1975 - APL 1-0873

(58) "Pure Gold" - 1975 - ANL 1-0873

(59) "Today" - 1975 - ANL 1-1039

(60) "The Sun Sessions" - 1975 - APM 1-1675

(61) "His Hand In Mine" - 1976 - ANL 1-1319

(62) "Elvis, Volume 2 - A Legendary Performer" - 1976 - CPL 1-1239

(63) "From Elvis Presley Boulevard, Memphis, Tennessee" - 1976 - APL 1-1506

(64) "Elvis Sings 'The Wonderful World of Christmas'" - 1976 - ANL 1-1936

(65) "Welcome To My World" - 1977 - APL 1-2274

(66) "Moody Blue" - 1977 - AFL 1-2347

Not all of the above albums will be available in record stores today, but the list should be helpful in placing orders for Elvis albums that seem particularly interesting.

The listing that follows provides the names of every song on all of Elvis' most important LPs. By consulting this directory of album cuts you can identify those LPs that contain the material by Elvis that you most like. All of Elvis' albums—which are also available on stereo eight track and/or cassette tapes—are on RCA Records.

(1) "ELVIS PRESLEY" — Blue Suede Shoes; I'm Counting On You; I'm Gonna Sit Right Down and Cry; I'll Never Let You Go; I Got A Woman; One Sided Love Affair; Tutti Fruitti; Tryin' To Get You; Just Because; I Love You Because; Blue Moon; Honey Honey. Also available on Stereo 8 tape. 1956. LSP 1254.

(2) "ELVIS" — Rip It Up; Love Me; Paralyzed; When My Blue Moon Turns To Gold; So Glad You're Mine; Old Shep; Ready Teddy; Any Place Is Paradise; Long Tall Sally; First In Line; How Do You Think I Feel; How's The World Treating You. Also available on Stereo 8 tape. 1956. LSP 1382.

(3) "LOVING YOU" — Loving You; Party; Teddy Bear; True Love; I Need You So; Lonesome Cowboy; Hot Dog; Got A Lot O'Lovin' To Do; Mean Woman Blues; Blueberry Hill; Don't Leave Now; Have I Told You Lately That I Love You. Also features the Jordanaires. Also available on Stereo 8 tape. 1957. LSP 1515.

187

(4) "ELVIS GOLDEN RECORDS" — Hound Dog; Loving You; All Shook Up; Love Me; Heartbreak Hotel; Jailhouse Rock; Too Much; Don't Be Cruel; That's When Your Heartaches Begin; Teddy Bear; Anyway You Want Me; Love Me Tender; Treat Me Nice; I Want You, I Need You, I Love You. Also available on Stereo 8 and cassette tapes. 1958. LSP 1707.

(5) "KING CREOLE" — King Creole; As Long As I Have You; Lover Doll; New Orleans; Trouble; Dixieland Rock; Crawfish; Young Dreams; Don't Ask Me Why; Hard Headed Woman; Steadfast, Loyal and True. Also available on Stereo 8 tape. 1958. LSP 1834.

(6) "FOR LP FANS ONLY" — That's All Right; Mystery Train; Lawdy, Miss Clawdy; Playing For Keeps; Poor Boy; My Baby Left Me; I Was The One; I'm Left, You're Right, She's Gone; Shake, Rattle & Roll; You're A Heartbreaker. Also available on Stereo 8 tape. 1959. LSP. 1990.

(7) "A DATE WITH ELVIS" — Blue Moon of Kentucky; Young and Beautiful; Baby I Don't Care; Milkcow Blues Boogie; Baby Let's Play House; We're Gonna Move; Good Rockin Tonight; Is It So Strange; I Want To Be Free; I Forgot To Remember To Forget. Also available on Stereo 8 tape. 1959. LSP 2011.

(8) "50,000,000 ELVIS FANS CAN'T BE WRONG — ELVIS' GOLD RECORDS, VOLUME

2" — I Need Your Love Tonight; Don't; Wear My Ring Around Your Neck; My Wish Came True; I Got Stung; One Night; Big Hunk O'Love; I Beg Of You; Fool Such As I; Doncha' Think It's Time. Also available on Stereo 8 tape. 1959. LSP 2075.

(9) "ELVIS IS BACK!" — Make Me Know It; Fever; Girl Of My Best Friend; I Will Be Home Again; Dirty, Dirty Feeling; Thrill Of Your Love; Soldier Boy; Such A Night; It Feels So Right; Girl Next Door; Like A Baby; Reconsider, Baby. Also available on Stereo 8 tape. 1960. LSP 2231.

(10) "G.I. BLUES" — Tonight Is So Right For Love; What's She Really Like; Frankfort Special; Wooden Heart; G.I. Blues; Pocketful Of Rainbows; Shoppin' Around; Big Boots; Didja' Ever; Blue Suede Shoes; Doin' The Best I Can. Also available on Stereo 8 and cassette tapes. 1960. LSP 2256.

(11) "HIS HAND IN MINE" — His Hand In Mine; In My Father's House; I'm Gonna Walk Dem Golden Stairs; If We Never Meet Again; Milky White Way; I Believe In The Man In The Sky; Known Only To Him; He Knows Just What I Need; Joshua Fit The Battle; Swing Down Sweet Chariot; Mansion Over The Hilltop; Working On The Building. Also available on Stereo 8 and cassette tapes. 1960. LSP 2328.

(12) "SOMETHING FOR EVERYBODY" — There's Always Me; Give Me The Right; It's A Sin; Sentimental Me; Starting Today; I'm Comin' Home; Gently; In Your Arms; Put The Blame On Me; Judy; I

Want You With Me; I Slipped, I Stumbled I Fell. Also available on Stereo 8 and cassette tapes. 1961. LSP 2370.

(13) "BLUE HAWAII" — Blue Hawaii; Almost Always True; No More' Aloha Oe; Can't Help In Love; Rock-a-Hula Baby; Moonlight Swim; Ku-U-I Po; Ito Eats; Slicin' Sand; Hawaiian Sunset; Beach Boy Blues; Island Of Love; Hawaiian Wedding Song. Also available on Stereo 8 and cassette tapes. 1961. LSP 2426.

(14) "POT LUCK" — Kiss Me Quick; Just For Old Time Sake; Easy Question; Gonna Get Back Home Somehow; I'm Yours; Steppin' Out Of LIne; I Feel That I've Known You Forever; Night Rider; Fountain Of Love; That's Someone You Never Forget. Also available on Stereo 8 tape. 1962. LSP 2523.

(15) "GIRLS! GIRLS! GIRLS!" — Girls, Girls, Girls; I Don't Wanna Be Tied; Where Do You Come From; I Don't Want To; We'll Be Together; Boy Like Me, A Girl Like You; Earth Boy; Return to Sender; Because of Love; Thanks To The Rolling Sea; Song Of The Shrimp; Walls Have Ears; We're Coming In Loaded. Also available on Stereo 8 tape. 1962. LSP 2621.

(16) "FUN IN ACAPULCO" — Fun In Acapulco; Vico, Dinero Y Amor; Toro; Mexico; Marguerita; No Room To Rhumba In A Sports Car; Bullfighter Was A Lady; Love Me Tonight; I Think I'm Gonna Like It Here; You Can't Say No In Acapulco; Bossa Nova, Baby; Guadalajara; Slowly But Surely. Also available

on Stereo 8 tape. 1963. LSP 2756.

(17) "ELVIS GOLDEN RECORDS, VOLUME 3" — It's Now Or Never; Stuck On You; Fame and Fortune; Surrender; I Gotta Know; I Feel So Bad; Are You Lonesome Tonight; Little Sister; Latest Flame; Good Luck Charm; Anything That's Part Of You; She's Not You. Also available on Stereo 8 and cassette tapes. 1963. LSP 2765.

(18) "KISSIN' COUSINS" — Kissin' Cousins; Kissin' Cousins No. 2; One Boy and Two Girls; Smokey Mountain Boy; Long Lonely Highway; There's Gold In The Mountains; Catchin' On Fast; Anyone; Once Is Enough; Tender Feeling; Barefoot Ballad; Echoes Of Love. Also available on Stereo 8 tape. 1964. LSP 2894.

(19) "ROUSTABOUT" — Roustabout; Little Egypt; Hard Knocks; Big Love, Big Heartache; Poison Ivy League; It's A Wonderful World; One Track Heart; Carny-Town; It's Carnival Time; There's A Brand New Day On The Horizon; Wheels On My Heels. Also available on ·Stereo 8 tape. 1964. LSP 2999.

(20) "GIRL HAPPY" — Girl Happy; Spring Fever; Fort Lauderdale Chamber of Commerce; Startin' Tonight; Do Not Disturb; Wolf Call; Cross My Heart and Hope To Die; Meanest Girl In Town; Do The Clam; Puppet On A String; I've Got To Find My Baby; You'll Be Gone. Also available on Stereo 8 and cassette tapes. 1965. LSP 3338.

(21) "ELVIS FOR EVERYONE" — Your Cheatin' Heart; Tomorrow Night; When It Rains, It Really Pours; Summer Kisses, Winter Tears; Finders Keepers, Losers Weepers; In My Way; Forget Me Never; For The Millionth and The Last Time; Memphis, Tennessee; Sound Advice; Santa Lucia; I Met Her Today. Also available on Stereo 8 and cassette tapes. 1965. LSP 3450.

(22) "PARADISE, HAWAIIAN STYLE" — Paradise, Hawaiian Style; Queenie Wahine's Papaya; Scratch My Back; Datin'; Drums Of The Islands; Dog's Life; House Of Sand; Stop Where You Are; This Is My Heaven; Sand Castles. Also available on Stereo 8 and cassette tapes. 1966. LSP 3643.

(23) "ELVIS' GOLD RECORDS, VOLUME 4" — Love Letters; Witchcraft; It Hurts Me; Ask Me; What'd I Say; Please Don't Drag That String Around; Indescribably Blue; You're The Devil In Disguise; Lonely Man; Mess Of Blues; Ain't That Loving You Baby; Just Tell Her Jim Said Hello. Also available on Stereo 8 and cassette tapes. 1968. LSP 3921.

(24) "SPEEDWAY" — There Ain't Nothing Like A Song; Your Groovy Self (by Nancy Sinatra); Speedway; Your Time Hasn't Come Yet, Baby; Who Are You; He's Your Uncle Not Your Dad; Let Yourself Go; Five Sleepyheads; Western Union; Mine; Going Home; Suppose. Also featuring Nancy Sinatra. Also available on Stereo 8 and cassette tapes. 1968. LSP 3989.

(25) "ELVIS — TV SPECIAL" — Trouble; Guitar

Man; Lawdy Miss Clawdy; Baby What You Want Me To Do; Heartbreak Hotel; Hound Dog; All Shook Up; Can't Help Falling In Love; Jailhouse Rock; Love Me Tender; Where Could I Go But To The Lord; Saved; Blue Christmas; One Night; Big Boss Man; Memories; Nothingsville; If I Can Dream; Little Egypt; Medley. Also available on Stereo 8 and cassette tapes. 1968. LSP 4088.

(26) "ELVIS SINGS FLAMING STAR AND OTHERS" — Flaming Star; Night Life; Do The Vega; Tiger Man; plus five other selections. Not available on tape. 1969. CAS 2304.

(27) "FROM ELVIS IN MEMPHIS" — Wearin' That Loved On Look; I'll Hold You In My Heart; Only The Strong Survive; Power of My Love; Long Black Limousine; Gentle On My Mind; It Keeps Right On A-Hurtin'; I'm Movin' On; After Loving You; Any Day Now; True Love Travels A Gravel Road; In The Ghetto. Also available on Stereo 8, Q8 and cassette tapes. 1969. LSP 4155.

(28) "FROM MEMPHIS TO VEGAS/FROM VEGAS TO MEMPHIS" — Blue Suede Shoes; Johnny B. Good; All Shook Up; Are You Lonesome Tonight; Hound Dog; I Can't Stop Loving You; My Baby; Words; In The Ghetto; Suspicious Minds; Can't Help Falling In Love; Inherit The Wind; This Is The Story; Stranger In My Own Home Town; Little Bit Of Green; Do You Know Who I Am; From A Jack To A King; Fair's Moving on; You'll Think Of Me; Without Love; Medley. Also available on Stereo 8 tape. 1969. LSP 6020.

(29) **"ON STAGE (FEBRUARY, 1970)"** — See See Rider, Release Me; Sweet Caroline; Runaway; Wonder Of You; Polk Salad Annie; Yesterday; Proud Mary; Walk A Mile In My Shoes; Let It Be Me. Also featuring The Imperials Quartet. Also available on Stero 8, Q8 and cassette tapes. 1970. LSP 4362.

(30) **"ELVIS IN PERSON AT THE INTERNATIONAL HOTEL, LAS VEGAS, NEVADA"** — Blue Suede Shoes; Johnny B. Good; All Shook Up; Are You Lonesome Tonight; Hound Dog; I Can't Stop Loving You; My Babe; Words; In The Ghetto; Suspicious Minds; Can't Help Falling In Love; Medley. Not available on tape. 1970. LSP 4428.

(31) **"ELVIS BACK IN MEMPHIS"** — Inherit The Wind; This Is The Story; Little Bit Of Green; Stranger In My Own Home Town; And The Grass Won't Pay No Mind; Do You Know Who I Am; From A Jack To A King; Fair's Moving On; You'll Think Of Me; Without Love. Also available on Stereo 8 and cassette tapes. 1970. LSP 4429.

(32) **"ELVIS — THAT'S THE WAY IT IS"** — I Just Can't Help Believin'; Twenty Days and Twenty Nights; How The Web Was Woven; I've Lost You; Patch It Up; Mary In The Morning; You Don't Have To Say You Love Me; You've Lost That Lovin' Feelin'; Just Pretend; Stranger In The Crowd; Next Step Is Love; Bridge Over Troubled Water. Also available on Stereo 8, Q8 and cassette

tapes. 1970. LSP 4445.

(33) "ELVIS' WORLDWIDE 50 GOLD AWARD HITS, Volume One" — Heartbreak Hotel; I Was The One; Hound Dog; I Want You, I Need You, I Love You; Don't Be Cruel; Love Me Tender; Anyway You Want Me; Too Much; Playing For Keeps; I'm All Shook Up; That's When Your Heartaches Begin; Loving You; Teddy Bear; Jailhouse Rock; Treat Me Nice; I Beg Of You; Don't Wear My Ring Around Your Neck; Fool Such As I; Hard Headed Woman; I Got Stung; Big Hunk O'Love; Stuck On You; Mess of Blues; It's Now Or Never; I Gotta Know; Are You Lonesome Tonight; Surrender; I Feel So Bad; Little Sister; Can't Help Falling In Love; Rock-a-Hula Baby; Anything That's Part Of You; Good Luck Charm; She's Not You; Return to Sender; Where Do You Come From; One Broken Heart For Sale; You're The Devil In Disguise; Bossa Nova Baby; Kissin' Cousins; Viva Las Vegas; Ain't That Loving You Baby; Wooden Heart; Crying In The Chapel; If I Can Dream; In The Ghetto; Suspicious Minds; Don't Cry Daddy; Kentucky Man; Plus excerpts from "Elvis Sails." Four record set. Also available on Stereo 8 and cassette tapes. 1970. LPM 6401

(34) "ELVIS COUNTRY" — Also known as "I'M 10,000 YEARS OLD" — Snowbird; Tomorrow Never Comes; Little Cabin On The Hill; Whole Lotta Shakin' Goin On; Funny How Time Slips Away; I Really Don't Want To Know; It's Your Baby, You Rock It; There Goes My Everything; Fool; Faded Love; I Washed My Hands In Muddy

Water; Make The World Go Away. Also available on Stereo 8 and cassette tapes. 1971. LSP 4460.

(35) "LOVE LETTERS FROM ELVIS" — Love Letters; When I'm Over You; If I Were You; Got My Mojo Working; Heart Of Rome; Only Believe; This Is Our Dance; Cindy, Cindy; I'll Never Know; It Ain't No Big Thing; Life. Also available on Stereo 8 and cassette tapes. 1971. LSP 4530.

(36) "ELVIS — THE OTHER SIDE — WORLDWIDE GOLD AWARD HITS, Volume 2" — Puppet On A String; Witchcraft; Trouble; I Want To Be Free; Poor Boy; Doncha' Think It's Time; Young Dreams; Next Step Is Love; You Don't Have To Say You Love Me; My Wish Came True; Paralyzed; When My Blue Moon Turns To Gold Again; Lonesome Cowboy; Tell Me Why; My Baby Left Me; It Hurts Me; King Creole; I Need Your Love Tonight; Please Don't Drag That String Around; Hot Dog; New Orleans; Young and Beautiful; We're Gonna Move; Crawfish; I Believe In The Man In The Sky; Dixieland Rock; Wonder Of You; They Remind Me Too Much Of You; Mean Woman Blues; Lonely Man; Any Day Now; Don't Ask Me Why; His Latest Flame; I Really Don't Want To Know; Baby, I Don't Care; I've Lost You; Let Me; Love Me; Got A Lot O'Livin' To Do; Fame and Fortune; Rip It Up; There Goes My Everything; Lover Doll; One Night; Just Tell Her Jim Said Hello; Ask Me; Patch It Up; As Long As I Have You; You'll Think of Me; Wild In The Country. Not available on tape. Four record set. 1971. LPM 6402.

(37) "ELVIS NOW" — Help Me Make It Through The Night; Miracle Of The Rosary; Hey Jude; Put Your Hand In The Hand; Until It's Time For You To Go; We Can Make The Morning; Early Mornin' Rain; Sylvia; Fools Rush In; I Was Born About Ten Thousand Years Ago. Also available on Stereo 8 and cassette tapes. 1972. LSP 4671.

(38) "HE TOUCHED ME" — He Touched Me; I've Got Confidence; Seeing Is Believing; Amazing Grace; He Is My Everything; Bosom Of Abraham; Evening Prayer; Lead Me, Guide Me; There Is No God But God; Thing Called Love; I, John; Reach Out To Jesus. Also available on Stereo 8 and cassette tapes. 1972. LSP 4690.

(39) "ELVIS AS RECORDED LIVE AT MADISON SQUARE GARDEN" — Introduction: Also Sprach Zarathustra; For The Good Times; That's All Right; You Don't Have To Say You Love Me; Proud Mary; Never Been To Spain; You've Lost That Lovin' Feelin'; Polk Salad Annie; Love Me; Hound Dog; All Shook Up; Heartbreak Hotel; Can't Help Falling In Love; Impossible Dream; I Can't Stop Loving You; Suspicious Minds; Introductions by Elvis Presley; Medley. Also available on Stereo 8, Q8 and cassette tapes. 1972. LSP 4776.

(40) "FOOL" — Fool; Where Do I Go From Here; It's Still Here; It's Impossible; I Will Be True; I'll Take You Home Again Kathleen; That's What You Get For Loving Me; Padre; Don't Think Twice; It's All Right; Love Me; Love The Life I

Lead. Not available on tape. 1973. APL 1-0283.

(41) "ELVIS, VOLUME 1 — A LEGENDARY PERFORMER" — That's All Right; I Love You Because; Don't Be Cruel; Heartbreak Hotel; Love Me; Love Me Tender; Trying To Get To You; Peace In The Valley; Fool Such As I; Tonight's All Right For Love; Are You Lonesome Tonight?; Can't Help Falling In Love; Excerpts from 9/22/58 interview. Also available on Stereo 8 and cassette tapes. 1973. CP1 1-0341.

(42) "RAISED ON ROCK" — Raised on Rock; For Ol' Times Sake; Are You Sincere; Find Out What's Happening; I Miss You; Girl Of Mine; If You Don't Come Back; Sweet Angeline; Three Corn Patches; Just A Little Bit. Not available on tape. 1973. APL 1-0388.

(43) "ELVIS — ALOHA FROM HAWAII VIA SATELLITE" — See See Rider; Burning Love; Something; My Way; You Gave Me A Mountain; Steamroller Blues; Love Me; Johnny B. Good; It's Over; Blue Suede Shoes; I'm So Lonesome I Could Cry; I Can't Stop Loving You; Hound Dog; Big Hunk Of Love; What Now My Love; Fever; Welcome To My World; Suspicious Minds; I'll Remember You; American Trilogy; Can't Help Falling In Love; Medley. Also available on Stereo 8, Q8 and cassette tapes, and on Quadradisk. 1973. VPSX 6089.

(44) "GOOD TIMES" — Take Good Care Of Her; Loving Arms; I Got A Feelin' In My Body; If

That Isn't Love; She Wears My Ring; I've Got A Thing About You Baby; My Boy; Spanish Eyes; Talk About The Good Times; Good Time Charlie's Got The Blues. Not available on tape. 1974. CPL 1-0475.

(45) "HAVING FUN WITH ELVIS ON STAGE" — Ad libs with audience; plus cuts included in more extensive LP set "ELVIS — THE OTHER SIDES — WORLDWIDE GOLD AWARD HITS, Volume 2." Also available on Stereo 8 and cassette tapes. 1974. CPM 1-0818.

(46) "ELVIS AS RECORDED LIVE ON STAGE IN MEMPHIS" — See See Rider; I Got A Woman; Blueberry Hill; Why Me Lord; Love Me; Trying To Get To You; My Baby Left Me; How Great Thou Art; Help Me; Let Me Be There; American Trilogy; Lawdy, Miss Clawdy; Can't Help Falling In Love; I Can't Stop Loving You; Rock Medley; Closing — Vamp. Not available on tape. 1974. CPL 1-0606.

(47) "PROMISED LAND" — Promised Land; There's A Honky Tonk Angel; You Asked Me To; Help Me; Mr. Songman; Love Song Of The Year; It's Midnight; Your Love's Been A Long Time Coming; If You Talk In Your Sleep; Thinking About You. Also available on Stereo 8, Q8 and cassette tapes and on Quadradisk. 1975. APL 1-0873.

(48) "PURE GOLD" — Love Me Tender; Loving You; Kentucky Rain; Fever; It's Impossible;

Jailhouse Rock; All Shook Up; Don't Be Cruel; I Got A Woman; In The Ghetto. Also available on Stereo 8 and cassette tapes. 1975. ANL 1-0971.

(49) "TODAY" — T-R-O-U-B-L-E; And I Love You So; I Can't Help; Fairytale; Susan When She Tried; Woman Without Love; Shake A Hand; Pieces Of My Life; Bringin' It Back; Green Green Grass of Home. Also available on Stereo 8, Q8 and cassette tapes and on Quadradisk.

(50) "THE SUN SESSIONS" — That's All Right; Good Rockin' Tonight; I Love You Because; Just Because; Blue Moon; Blue Moon Of Kentucky; I Don't Care If The Sun Don't Shine; Milkcow Blues Boogie; I'm Left, You're Right, She's Gone; You're A Heartbreaker; Baby Let's Play House; I'll Never Let You Go; Mystery Train; I Forgot To Remember To Forget; Trying To Get To You. Also available on Stereo 8 and cassette tapes. 1975. APM 1-1675.

(51) "HIS HAND IN MINE" — His Hand In Mine; In My Father's House; I'm Gonna Walk Dem Golden Stairs; If We Never Meet Again; Milky White Way; I Believe In The Man In The Sky; Known Only To Him; He Knowns Just What I Need; Joshus Fit The Battle; Swind Down Sweet Chariot; Mansion Over The Hilltop; Working On The Building. Also available on Stereo 8 tape. 1976. ANL 1-1319.

(52) "ELVIS, VOLUME 2 — A LEGENDARY PERFORMER" — Harbor Lights; I Want You, I Need You, I Love You; Blue Suede Shoes; Jailhouse

Rock; Blue Christmas; It's Now Or Never; Cane and A High Starched Collar; Blue Hawaii; Such A Night; Baby What You Want Me To Do; How Great Thou Art; If I Can Dream; Interview; Presentations Of Awards To Elvis. Also available on Stereo 8 and cassette tapes. 1976. CPL 1-1349.

(53) "FROM ELVIS PRESLEY BOULE-VARD, MEMPHIS, TENNESSEE" — Hurt; Never Again; Blue Eyes Crying In The Rain; Danny Boy; Last Farewell; For The Heart; Bitter They Are, Harder They Fall; Solitaire; Love Coming Down; I'll Never Fall In Love Again. Recorded live. Also available on Stereo 8 and cassette tapes. 1976. APL 1-1506.

(54) "MOODY BLUE" — Moody Blue; She Thinks I Still Care; Way Down; Pledging My Love; It's Easy For You; Let Me Be There; If You Love Me Let Me Know; He'll Have To Go; Unchained Melody; Little Darlin'. Also available on Stereo 8 and cassette tapes. 1977. AFL 1-2347.

# CHAPTER NINE

## AN ELVIS FILMOGRAPHY

*"The death of no star has provoked
this kind of interest in films," Seth
Willenson of Films, Inc. declared.*

In his lifetime Elvis Presley starred in 33 motion
pictures, which are estimated to have grossed over
$150 million at box-offices around the world. From
his first picture, "Love Me Tender" in 1956, right
through to the last documentary about him, "Elvis
on Tour" in 1972, Elvis had an enormous following
of dedicated fans who supported any picture he
made. While the quality of Elvis' films varied, some
being substantially better than others, his fans
seemed to enjoy them all. Releasing an Elvis Presley
movie was like having money in the bank.

At the time of Elvis' death there were about 100
prints of his feature films available for theatrical
distribution. Some of them were 35mm prints and
some were less desirable 16mm prints. The
companies that specialize in distribution of classic
or semi-classic pictures quickly put together Elvis
festivals or collections of as many Elvis films as they
could get their hands on.

Films, Inc., one of the biggest distributors of
products for the nontheatrical market—colleges,
military, and other specialized showings—immed-

iately booked about 25 Elvis festivals on college campuses.

"I've never seen this kind of translation from public event to 16mm film rental," Seth Willenson, Vice President and National Sales Manager for Films, Inc., was quoted as saying.

"In my 10 years in sales, the death of no star has provoked this kind of interest in films," he added. That, presumably, included the tragic death in 1962 of Marilyn Monroe.

The owner and operator of Chicago's Biograph Theatre, which specializes in revivals of classic films, noted that, "There are more Elvis fans in Chicago than anyone ever dreamed." Larry Edwards went on to explain that, "I think that the movie experience will be a sort of public mourning—people wanting to congregate in one room to share the experience."

In all, Elvis made a total of 33 pictures. The complete filmography that follows may well be the only comprehensive source for data about these movies.* The filmography is presented in alphabetical order to make it easier to locate specific titles that may be of interest to the reader.

In chronological order, Elvis' motion pictures were:

   (1)   "Love Me Tender"-1956
   (2)   "Loving You"-1957
   (3)   "Jailhouse Rock"-1957
   (4)   "King Creole"-1958
   (5)   "G.I. Blues"-1960
   (6)   "Flaming Star"-1960
   (7)   "Wild In The Country"-1961
   (8)   "Blue Hawaii"-1961

(9)  "Kid Galahad"-1962
(10) "Girls, Girls, Girls"-1962
(11) "Follow That Dream-1962

*Special thanks for assistance and cooperation in preparing the following filmography must go to the library staff of the Academy of Motion Picture Arts & Sciences in Beverly Hills, California.*

(12) "Fun In Acapulco"-1963
(13) "It Happened At The World's Fair"-1963
(14) "Kissin' Counsins"-1964
(15) "Viva Las Vegas"-1964
(16) "Roustabout"-1964
(17) "Girl Happy"-1965
(18) "Tickle Me"-1965
(19) "Harum Scarum"-1965
(20) "Frankie and Johnny"—1966
(21) "Paradise Hawaiian Style"-1966
(22) "Spinout"-1966
(23) "Easy Come, Easy Go"-1967
(24) "Double Trouble"-1967
(25) "Stay Away Joe"-1968
(26) "Speedway"-1968
(27) "Clambake"-1968
(28) "Live A Little, Love A Little"-1968
(29) "Charro"-1969
(30) "Change of Habit"-1970
(31) "The Trouble With Girls"-1970
(32) "Elvis—That's The Way It is"-1970
(33) "Elvis on Tour"-1972

(1)  "BLUE HAWAII" — A Paramount Re-

lease. Produced by Hal Wallis. Directed by Norman Taurog. Associate Producer: Paul Nathan. Screenplay: Hal Kanter. Photography: Charles Lang, Jr. Art direction: Walter Tyler. Set decoration: Sam Comer, Frank McKelvy. Music: Joseph J. Lilley. Sound: Phil Mitchel. Film editor: Warren Low. Assistant director: Mickey Moore. Filmed in Technicolor and Panavision. Running time: 103 minutes.

*CAST:* Elvis Presley, Joan Blackman, Nancy Walters, Roland Winters, Angela Lansbury, John Archer, Howard McNear, Flora Hayes, Gregory Gay, Steve Brodie, Iris Adrian, Darlene Tompkins, Pamela Akert, Christian Kay, Jenny Maxwell, Frank Atienza, Lani Kai, Joss De Varga and Ralph Hanalie.

Elvis played the role of Chad Gates, son of a rich pineapple grower who want to make good on his own.

*Reviews: Variety's* reviewer, *Tube,* gave "Blue Hawaii" generally good marks (11/29/61). He said it "restores Elvis Presley to his natural screen element—the romantic, non-cerebral film-musical," noting that Elvis' past few pictures had been heavier dramas. Writing that this was the "sort of vehicle which the singing star seems to enjoy his greatest popularity in, the kind his vast legion of fans seems to prefer him in," he predicted that the movie should do well at the box office.

In The Hollywood *Reporter* James Powers wrote (11/24/61) that the film "is for the Elvis Presley fans. A new setting to exploit the popular singer's appeal." He also found that Elvis "handles himself with his usual adroitness, although he has a tendency to fall out of character."

In Motion Picture *Herald* (11/29/61) James D. Ivers summed it up this way: "Exhibitors for whom Elvis Presley's name is marquee magic (and where in all the land is it not?) need know no more about this film than that it is all Presley from start to finish. The swivel-hipped young man with the irresistible appeal sings 14 songs, strums a ukelele, dances the primitive form of the Twist, and charms the ladies, young and old, through every foot of the production." He added that theatres playing the picture have "Box office insurance of a kind not often found these days."

In October 1962 "Blue Hawaii" was due to open in Mexico City. But the Mexican government prevented that, saying that it was banning all Elvis Presley films. This was said to stem from the fact that Elvis' fans rioted during an earlier Mexican showing of "G.I. Blues." The theatre in which that picture was shown suffered torn up seats, broken windows and other damage.

Subsequently, Elvis and Mexico patched things up. In 1963 Elvis' film "Fun In Acapulco," which depicted Mexico most favorably, was released in the U.S. Elvis' pictures were, once again, welcome south of the border!

(2) "CHANGE OF HABIT" — A Universal Release. Produced by Joe Connelly. Directed by William Graham. Associate producer: Irving Paley. Screenplay: James Lee and S.S. Schweitzer, Eric Bercovici. Based on a story by John Joseph and Richard Morris. Photography: Russell Metty. Art

direction: Alexander Golitzen. Music: Ben Weisman. Songs: Buddy Kaye, Ben Weisman. Music supervision: Stanley Wilson. Sound: Waldon O. Watson, Lyle Cain, Ronald Pierce. Film editor: Douglas Stewart. Filmed in Technicolor. Running time: 93 minutes. MPAA rating: G/general audiences.

*Cast:* Elvis Presley, Mary Tyler Moore, Barbara McNair, Jane Elliot, Leora Dana, Edward Asner, Robert Emhardt, Regis Toomey, Doro Merande, Ruth McDevitt, Richard Carlson, Nefti Millet, Laura Figueroa, Lorena Kirk, Virginia Vincente, David Renard, Ti-Tu Cumbuka, Bill Elliott, Rodolfo Hoyos and Timothy Carey.

Elvis played the role of Dr. John Carpenter, and Mary Tyler Moor was cast as a nun, Sister Michelle.

*Reviews: Variety's* reviewer, *Whit,* thought Elvis was "strongly cast" and "displays his customary easy presence" (10/22/69). He also found that "Miss Moore delivers a spritely performance." He noted that Elvis only sang two songs in the picture, and that this was in keeping with his recent direction toward more dramatic films.

In the Los Angeles *Times* (11/20/69) Kevin Thomas didn't care much for the picture, but thought Elvis "is especially good, even at time making you forget it's he whom you're watching. If only Presley would dare to move on to something completely new—he might have been terrific in the Glen Campbell role in 'True Grit'."

As for the film, Thomas noted, "Today we are simply too aware how agonizing social injustices can be for them to be treated with the breezy, jaunty touch of simple-minded light comedy."

Whereas Elvis had romped through earlier films, in "Change of Habit" he was cast as a doctor running a ghetto clinic with the help of some nuns. It was a much heavier role for him to handle.

John Goff of The Hollywood *Reporter* (10/17/69) called the film, "something of a departure from the beaten path of Elvis Presley movies." He thought it might not "please a great deal of his fans" that Elvis was singing less on screen. And he concluded, "It will take a gentle leading of his fans into the new bag, that of a man who has seen the last of his twenties, but with slight changes in each future film as in this one perhaps a new Presley will emerge."

(3) "CHARRO!" — A National General Pictures release. Executive producer: Harry Caplan. Produced, directed and written by Charles Marquis Warren. Story by Frederic Louis Fox. Photography: Ellsworth Fredericks. Art direction: James Sullivan. Set decoration: Charles Thompson. Music: Hugo Montenegro. Sound: Urey Kauk. Film editor: Al Clark. Associate producer/director: Dink Templeton. Filmed in Technicolor and Panavision. Running time: 98 minutes. MPAA rating G/general audiences.

*Cast:* Elvis Presley, Ina Balin, Victor French, Lynn Kellog, Barbara Werle, Solomon Sturges, Paul Brinegar, James Sikking, Harry Landers, Tony Young, James Almanzar, Charles H. Gray. Rod Redwing, Gary Walberg, Duane Grey, J. Edward McKinley, John Pickard, Robert Luster, Christa Lang, Robert Karnes.

Elvis played the role of Jess Wade, an ex-outlaw

who saves a town from his old gang buddies.

*Reviews:* "Charro!" was not one of Elvis' better regarded pictures. *Variety's* Robe. (3/12/69) called it a "minor effort," and explained that "the latest attempt by Presley to become an actor, rather than a singer, is to stroll through a tedious role that would have driven any serious actor up the wall."

Mandel Herbstman was somewhat kinder in *Film/Television Daily (3/14/69), saying that, "while the picture is not one of dramatic distinction it does provide excellent fare in its category."*

*The Hollywood Reporter's* John Mahoney complained that, "with a lesser draw and talent than Presley's going for it, it would be little more than a non-rating segment of a weekly television western grind."

Mahoney also pointed out that, "Few performers have managed to prevail and profit for as long at the mercy of such consistently tepid writing and direction as Elvis Presley. Nonetheless, Presley manages to the maximum of his abilities to turn in consistently credible and understanding performances which transcend the minimum demands of the budget packages which keep him in circulation."

(4) "CLAMBAKE" — A United Artists release. Produced by Jules Levy, Arthur Gardner and Arnold Laven. Directed by Arthur H. Nadel. Associate producer: Tom Rolf. Screenplay: Arthur Browne Jr. Photography: William Margulies. Art direction: Lloyd Papez. Set decoration: James Red. Music: Jeff Alexander. Sound: Frank Wilkinson. Film editor: Tom Rolf. Assistant directors: Claude Binyan Jr. and Bill Green. Filmed in Technicolor

and techniscope. Running time: 99 minutes.

*Cast:* Elvis Presley, Shelley Fabares, Will Hutchins, Bill Bixby, James Gregory, Gary Merill, Amanda Harley, Suzie Kaye, Angelique Pettyjohn, Olga Kaya, Arlene Charles, Jack Good, Hal Peary, Sam Riddle, Sue England, Lisa Slagel, Lee Drieger, Melvin Allen, Herb Barnett, Steve Cory, Robert Lieb and Red West.

Elvis was cast as Scott Heywad a rich man's son who trades identities with Will Hutchins because he doesn't want his father's money to be the reason girls fall for him.

*Reviews: Variety's* reviewer, *Whit,* liked "Clambake" very much. "Elvis Presley has the benefit of superior mounting throughout," he wrote. The picture "is one of the singer's top offerings to date, backed by a legitimately premised story line, melodic songs, acceptable acting and singing with a spectacular water race." In his opinion the movie had "all the makings of beings one of Presley's heaviest grossers."

Kevin Thomas, who reviewed the film for the Los Angeles *Times* (11/1/67), didn't agree. He found that "the production numbers are more elaborate than usual, but Elvis' songs are as forgettable as ever, and the whole picture has a garish, cluttered look." He also thought that while "Clambake" was "pleasant and unpretentious" it has a "synthetic appearance. The starlets look lacuered, the set plasticized and there's much reliance on process work." In The Hollywood *Reporter* (10/18/67) John Mahoney told readers that the film is "as good as prior Presley outings on a tight budget and should do well wherever such films are necessary fodder." He cited Elvis as "a natural and competent actor with the ability to add credible dimension to a rough sketch."

Looking to the future for Elvis, Mahoney wrote that he can't "continue for long to rely on the same scripts and songs which have become anachronistic in the increasingly sophisticated and ever-changing world of pop music and pulp films."

Motion Picture *Herald* critic Lowell Redelings called "Clambake" a "bright and bouncy package of all-around entertainment...in the genre of his production pattern which continues to prove popular with his youthful audiences. It should do as well as its predecessors, at the very least, in general situations."

(5) "DOUBLE TROUBLE" — An MGM release by Judd Bernard and Irwin Winkler. Directed by Norman Taurog. Screenplay: Jo Heims. Based on a story by Marc Brandel. Photography: Daniel L. Fapp. Art direction: George W. Davis and Merril Pye. Set decorations: Henry Grace and Hugh Hunt. Music: Jeff Alexander. Sound: Franklin Milton. Film editor: John McSweeney. Assistant director: Claude Binyon, Jr. Filmed in Metrocolor and Panavision. Running time: 91 minutes.

*Cast:* Elvis Presley, Annette Day, John Williams, Yvonne Roman, The Wier Brothers, Chips Rafferty, Norman Rossington, Monty Landis, Michael Murphy, Leon Askin, John Alderson, Stanley Adams, Maurice Marsac, Walter Burke, Helene Winston and The G Men.

Elvis was cast as Guy Lambert, an American

singer hitting discotheques throughout Europe.

*Reviews:* Variety (4/5/67) thought "Double Trouble" appeared to "have been whipped up to showcase a big name without much thought of content other than to serve as footage to cash in on the star's draw." The result, according to reviewer Whit, "is the sketchiest of story-line and treatment which leaves spectator wondering what it's all about." As for Elvis, "as usual, however, gives a pretty fair account of himself despite what's handed him."

The Los Angeles *Herald Examiner* (6/9/67) liked the picture, and pointed out that Elvis' "new vehicle affords the popular singing star ample opportunity to belt out nine songs. The story sees him in more of a straight acting role than previous films."

Mandel Herbstman, writing in *Film-Television Daily,* thought the movie was "handsomely mounted" though "formula styled for general audience appeal." He commented that it marks Presley's 24th picture and it rates well in comparison to predecessors."

In the Hollywood *Reporter* (4/5/67), John Mahoney called it "the most lavishly produced Elvis Presley film since 'Viva Las Vegas'" in 1964. He said it "boasts one of Presley's most tuneful and melodic scores, and again proves the singer's natural instinct for comedy." Elvis' performance, he wrote, was "an assured protrayal."

(6) "EASY COME, EASY GO" — A Paramount release. Produced by Hal Wallis. Directed by John Rich. Associate producer: Paul Nathan. Screenplay: Allan Weiss and Anthony Lawrence.

Photography: William Margulies. Underwater photography: Michael J. Dugan. Art direction: Hal Pereira and Walter Tyler. Set direction: Robert Benton and Arthur Krams. Music: Joseph J. Lilley. Sound: John Carter. Film editor: Archie Marshek. Assistant director: Robert Goldstein. Filmed in Technicolor. Running time: 96 minutes.

*Cast:* Elvis Presley, Dodie Marshall, Pat Priest, Pat Harrington, Skip Ward, Sandy Kenyon, Frank McHugh, Elsa Lanchester, Ed Griffith, Read Morgan, Mickey Elley, Elaine Beckett, Shari Nims, Diki Lerner, and Robert Isenberg.

Elvis played the role of Ted Jackson, a demolition expert in the U.S. Navy who finds sunken treasure off the coast of California and leaves the Navy to claim it for himself.

*Reviews: Variety's* critic *Murf.* (3/22/67), called it "another well-made Hal B. Wallis production," noting that it was the ninth that Elvis and Wallis had done together. He thought "Elvis looks great and ageless, although his maturity shows in the acting department."

*Murf.* observed that, "a generation from now, Elvis pix will be film festival items, just as the Busby Berkely, Astair-Rogers and Mae West pix are now."

Glen Hawkins review in the Los Angeles *Herald-Examiner* (3/24/67) ran under the headline "ELVIS AT HIS BEST." Calling Elvis "a darn good actor," Hawkins noted that the film differed from earlier efforts in that Elvis "isn't called upon to warble affectatiously in every other scene...The story is emphasized more. There's less strain on the ears."

*The Hollywood Reporter's* John Mahoney thought Elvis' fans would like the picture, which he called "a completely routine underwater treasure hunt." He noted that Elvis "is good, giving the role believability, good humor and personal style."

(7) "ELVIS ON TOUR" — An MGM release. Produced and directed by Pierre Adidge and Robert Abel. Technical advisor: Col. Tom Parker. Associate producer: Sidney Levin. Photography: Robert E. Thomas. Montage supervisor: Martin Scorcese. Film editor: Ken Zomke. Costumes: Bill Belew. Sound: James E. Webb Jr. Filmed in Metrocolor. Running time: 92 minutes. MPAA rating G/general audiences.

*Cast:* Elvis Presley in a documentary focusing on his activities on the concert circuit.

*Reviews:* Murf., in Variety (11/1/72), hailed the picture as "a bright, entertaining pop music documentary." He liked the "multi-panel composition and zesty editing," and made a point of noting that "Martin Scorsese's montage supervision highlights a top technical effort." Scorsese, some years later, became a noted director himself, turning out pictures such as "Mean Streets," "Alice Doesn't Live Here Anymore" and "Taxi Driver."

Kevin Thomas reviewed the picture favorably in the Los Angeles *Times,* finding it "as unpretentious as its title and therefore a lot more enjoyable than the 1970 Presley documentary, 'Elvis — That's The Way It Is.' "

In his review (1/17/73) Thomas also observed that, "Both offstage and on Presley comes across as an assured, relaxed, thoroughgoing pro who knows exactly what he's doing and enjoys it immensely."

Glen Lovell of The Hollywood *Reporter*

(11/2/72) was far less enthusiastic about the film. He said "it pours onto the screen as little more than an ambitious public relations tract," and complained that if offers no "new insights into the man."

Placing the blame for this at Col. Parker's feet, Lovell said he "apparently is continuing his efforts to insure that Elvis remain one of the most overpaid, underexposed performers in the business." He added that he thought Parker "was extra careful that no new facts, controversial or otherwise, be revealed."

He concluded that the film "will obviously have tremendous success with those committed-unto-death Presley disciples who accept the performer under any conditions. But for those anxiously awaiting a significant investigation which separates myth from fact and which does more than scratch obvious surface truths, there will be disappointment."

The New York *Times'* Vincent Canby wrote (6/17/73) that the film "strips away the storybook myth to find underneath a private person who is indistinguishable from the public one, except for the fact he dresses with somewhat less flamboyance.

"This could be the truth, but the film remains unconvincing. If it is true, then the stolid, nicely mannered Elvis we saw in all those dozens of Hal Wallis quickies is no more or less real than the actor who played the roles."

Canby concluded that "The person and the image have become one. For better or worse the camera has sanctified him."

*Films & Filming,* the distinguished British magazine of film criticism, devoted a long critique in its March 1973 issue to "Elvis On Tour." Alex Stuart arrived at a similar conclusion to Vincent Canby's in The New York *Times,* "it's difficult to distinguish between the public Elvis and the personal Elvis, if indeed anything of the personal is presented (if indeed it exists)."

Stuart explained that while the film "is a good feature on the strains of concert tours, the portrait of Elvis is glossy to the extent of seeming superficial. There is no attempt made to explain why he has 'lasted' when others have faded so rapidly from the scene, and why his popularity has, if anything, increased."

He wrote that the film shows that Elvis "hasn't changed: still the same implication with each twist of his body, the same oceans of sweat pouring from forehead and chest to be soaked up by the towel which at times gives him the appearance of an overgrown Linus. But surely he's just a little heavier in build, just a fraction older than he was a decade ago? Well, you try convincing an audience of middle-aged housewives and their daughters of that. For a start, the daughters probably don't even remember a decade back, and for their mothers to acknowledge that Elvis is aging they would have to think about a few home truths."

That, it seems, is a key point. For Elvis' audiences to perceive him as having aged, changed, matured, gotten older—whatever one chooses to call it—they must admit that they, too, have attained a new stage of life. That's an admission few people want to make about themselves, so it's best left unsaid or even unthought, where public figures like Elvis are concerned.

(8) "ELVIS — THAT'S THE WAY IT IS" — An MGM release. Produced by Herbert F. Solow. Directed by Denis Sanders. Photography: Lucien Ballard. Editor: Henry Berman. Sound: Larry Hadsell and Lyle Burbridge. Assistant director: John Wilson. Technical adviser: Col. Tom Parker. Filmed in Metrocolor and Panavision. Running time: 108 mnutes. MPAA rating: G/general audiences.

*Cast:* Elvis Presley stars in a documentary about his appearance at the International Hotel in Las Vegas in August 1970.

*Reviews: Daily Variety's Murf.* liked the picture very much. "Presley was the pied piper of the rock era," he wrote (10/27/70), "and this film shows that the parade hasn't even begun to pass him by." He added that "Presley explodes again on the screen," and called it a "handsomely and inventively assembled" Picture.

John Goff of The Hollywood *Reporter* (10/17/70) noted that Elvis "is perhaps the only performer today who will bring into movie theatres enough people to make a documentary of himself pay off for a major studio." He added that Elvis' fans "will go hoping to see something other than the fluff their idol has been churning out for these many years."

In Goff's view, "it isn't the usual fare, but neither is it quite the revealing portrait of the man they might hope it will be...But it is all Elvis and that's what the fans want and will be satisfied with."

Writing in The Los Angeles *Herald-Examiner,* Bridget Byrne cited it (12/9/70) as "a very inadequate documentary. Easy exploitation, stock sell stuff. A hack job by Denis Sanders. The camera follows but it does not penetrate. The director watches but does not comment or select."

As for Elvis, she agreed that he is "super and survives...He is a brilliant performer, a mammoth figure in pop music history. His timing is superb, his sense of line and form in his movement is superb." But her lament was that, "It is a shame that an opportunity has been missed to make more than just a film for fans...One day someone will actually put Elvis into a good movie, but they better do it quick before it's too late."

In *Films & Filming* (July 1971) Eric Braun noted that the film "reveals Presley as slimmer than before and never in better physical form." He complained that the interviews with fans in the movie detracted from its impact. "Fans are a very vulnerable breed of people," he said. "What may sound perfectly acceptable in private conversation becomes embarrassing when filmed for the millions. If Sanders has wished to show the Presley followers as morons he has succeeded admirably, even compounding the indignity by returning to clips from already unfortunate interviews during the star's actual concert performance."

Focusing on Elvis' film career, he observed, "It has been an astonishing career, unique only in the steadily declining quality of the vehicles meted out to one of the handful of excitingly original talents on the entertainment scene since the forties."

(9) "FLAMING STAR" — A Twentieth Century-Fox release. Produced by David Weisbart. Directed by Don Siegel. Screenplay Clair Huffaker

and Nunnally Johnson. Based on a novel by Clair Huffaker. Photography: Charles G. Clarke. Art direction: Duncan Cramer and Walter M. Simonds. Set direction: Walter M. Scott and Gustav Berntsen. Music: Cyril J. Mockridge. Sound: E. Clayton Ward and Warren B. Delaplain. Film editor: Hugh S. Fowler. Assistant director: Joseph E. Richards. Filmed in CinemaScope and Color by Deluxe. Running time: 92 minutes.

*Cast:* Elvis Presley, Steve Forrest, Barbara Eden, Dolores Del Rio, John McIntire, Rudolph Acosta, Karl Swenson, Ford Rainey, richard Jaeckel, Anne Benton, L.Q. Jones, Douglas Dick, Tom Reese, Marian Goldina, Monte Burkhart, Ten Jacques, Rod Redwing and Perry Lopez.

Elvis was cast in the role of Pacer, a half-Indian youth torn between his white father and Indian mother.

*Reviews:* Lynn Bowers of The Los Angeles *Examiner* found (12/22/60) that Elvis' "second picture since his liberation from the Army comes as an extremely pleasant surprise because it backs up the young star with a dramatically poignant story and a fine cast." She added that, "This picture should open up a whole new audience for him because of the adult theme and the strong support he is given."

The Hollywood *Reporter's* James Powers (12/19/60) decided that, "Taken as straight action melodrama it is first-rate entertainment, thanks chiefly to first-rate direction by Don Siegel. It will be justly popular with Presley fans and will also be palatable to those somewhat less fanatic about the singing star."

"Flaming Star" was the first Elvis movie in which he was "not portrayed as a singer," Lee Belser pointed out in a Los Angeles *Mirror* interview with director Don Siegel (11/30/60). In Siegel's opinion, Elvis is "electric!. He projects to the point where he jumps out at you from the screen. He had some of the same qualities as Rudolph Valentino. He has the same magnetism. But he's a much better actor."

Siegel also talked about how Elvis functioned as an actor. "Elvis didn't realize it, but he actually began using the Stanislavsky method. When he gets ready to do a serious scene, he closes himself in and is absolutely unapproachable to anyone but me." Siegel found him "very shy, very inhibited," and felt that "That is why he has his buddies around him all the time. Sometimes I found it difficult to get him away from them. There were things I had to explain to him and I couldn't do it in front of other people. Elvis has a very complex, but a very interesting personality."

As for the picture's songs, Siegel said that he originally "thought Elvis wanted the songs and he thought I wanted them. The truth is, neither of us wanted them and one day on the set we both blurted it out. From then on everything was fine."


(10) "FOLLOW THAT DREAM" — A United Artists release. Produced by David Weisbart. Directed by Gordon Douglas. Screenplay: Charles Lederer. Based on the novel "Pioneer, Go Home" by Richard Powell. Photography: Leo Tover. Art direction: Malcolm Bert. Set decoration: Fred McClean. Music: Hans J. Salter. Sound: Jack Solomon, Buddy Myers and Ruth Hancock. Film

editor: William B. Murphy. Assistant director: Bert Chervin. Filmed in Panavision and Color by DeLuxe. Running time 109 minutes.

*Cast:* Elvis Presley, Arthur O'Connell, Anne Helm, Joanna Moore, Jack Kruschen, Simon Oakland, Roland Winters, Alan Hewitt, Howard McNear, Frank de Kova, Herbert Rudley, Gavin and Robert Koon, Robert Carricart and John Duke.

Elvis was cast as Toby Kwinper, a young man whose problem is that girls won't leave him alone!

*Reviews:* In *Daily Variety* (3/28/62) *Tube.* suggested that "Presley buffs figure to take very kindly to the David Weisbart productin, which displays their hero in good form in the kind of vehicle in which the record shows him to be most salable—the light romantic comedy with songs." He also thought Elvis "conveys the right blend of horse sense and naivete in his characterization, and delivers five songs with vocal competence but nary a wiggle."

In The Hollywood *Reporter* (3/28/62) James Powers wrote that "Presley is not, of course, basically a comedian, but directed adroitly, as he is here, the laughs play about him and he comes off with disarming simplicity and sympathy."

Margaret Hartford reviewed the picture for The Los Angeles *Times* (4/20/62) and sighed "Ah, well, if Elvis will just ease up on the bread and potatoes, he can still keep American girlhood in swoons for a while."


(11) "FRANKIE AND JOHNNY" — A United Artists release. Produced by Edward Small.

Directed by Frederick de Cordova. Screenplay: Alex Gottlieb. Based on a story by Nat Perrin. Photography: Jacques Marquette. Music: Fred Karger. Film editor: Grant Whytock. Filmed in Technicolor. Running time: 87 minutes.

*Cast:* Elvis Presley, Donna Douglas, Harry Morgan, Sue Anne Langdon, Nancy Kovack, Audrey Christie, Robert Strauss, Anthony Eisley, Jerome Cowen, Wilda Taylor, Larri Thomas, Dee Jay Mattis and Judy Chapman.

Elvis played the title role of Johnny, a riverboat singer and gambler.

*Reviews: Variety's* Mitt. called it (3/30/66) "sure-fire boxoffice." He noted that "Elvis is Elvis. He sings and acts, apparently doing both with only slight effort. Presley does little hip swinging, no doubt in keeping with the period of the story."

The direction—by Fred De Cordova, now famous as producer of Johnny Carson's "Tonight" program—"gives a nice pace to the musical, helping to add to the easy-going relaxing mood of the whole thing," he commented.

Kevin Thomas wrote in The Los Angeles *Times* (5/27/66) that the film was "fast-moving fun" He saw it as "A pleasant, relaxing entertainment with 11 songs. It has an array of fine performances...and plenty of pulchritude in the delightful forms of Donna Douglas as Frankie and Nancy Kovack as Nellie Bly."

The Los Angeles *Herald-Examiner's* review by George H. Jackson observed that, "Good fortune continues to smile on Elvis Presley, who gets three luscious leading ladies for his newest movie musical."

(12) "FUN IN ACAPULCO" — A Parmount release. Produced by Hal Wallis. Directed by Richard thorpe. Screenplay: Allan Weiss. Photography: Daniel L. Fapp. Film editor: Stanley E. Johnson. Music: Joseph J. Lilley. Assistant director: Michael Moore. Running time: 100 minutes. Filmed in Technicolor.

*Cast:* Elvis Presley, Ursula Andress, Elsa Cardenas, Paul Lukas, Larry Domasin, Alejandro Rey, Robert Carricart, Teri Hope, Charles Evans, Alberto Mrin, Francisco Ortega, Robert De Anda, Linda Rivera, Darlene Tomkins, Linda Rand, Eddie Cano, Carlos Mejia, Leon Cardenas, Fred Aguirre, Tom Hernandez and Adele Palacios.

Elvis was cast as Mike Windgren, an out-of-work one-time high trapeze artist who has been stranded in Acapulco.

*Reviews:* In *Variety* (11/21/63) *Tube.* wrote that, "Presley has come a long way and is deserving of better material." But he noted that the "fans won't be disappointed—he sings ten servicable songs and wiggles a bit to boot. However the ground covered by the plot doesn't help to increase his star stature."

In *Film Daily* (11/21/63) Mandel Herbstman commented that the picture "is lighthearted and pleasant fun for the general patron." He thought "the production is mounted handsomely" and that "in general the film compares favorably with the previus Presley pictures."

The *Motion Picture Herald's* Richard Gertner noted (11/27/63) that "A successful pattern has been well established for most of the films of Elvis Presley, and that proven scheme is carefully adhered to in 'Fun In Acapulco.' This means the fans of the singer won't find many surprises in this new picture...but then they won't be disappointed either."

(13) "G.I. BLUES" — A Paramount release. Produced by Hal Wallis. Directed by Norman Taurog. Screenplay: Edmund Beloin and Henry Garson. Photography: Loyal Griggs. Film editor: Warren Low. Art direction: Hal Pereira and Walter Tyler. Music: Joseph J. Lilley. Running time: 115 minutes. Filmed in Technicolor.

*Cast:* Elvis presley, Juliet Prowse, Robert Ivers, Laticia Roman, James Douglas, Sigrid Maier and Arch Johnson.

Elvis played the role of Tulsa McCauley, as an Army tank gunner stationed in Germany where he discovers and goes after Juliet Prowse.

*Reviews:* "G.I. Blues" was Elvis' first picture after serving in the Army. *Variety's Tube* observed (10/19/60) that it "seems to have been left over from the frivolous filmusicals of World War II." He suggested that it would "have to depend on younger, pre-teen age groups for its chief response."

John L. Scott liked the film in the Los Angeles *Times* (11/16/60). He noted that the "snake-hips gyratios, fish-eye look and sullen attitude" were gone. He commented that, "I wouldn't actually call Elvis sophisticated in the picture, but he has grown up, for which we give thanks. And he's learning how to act, too, particularly in the lighter sequences."

How would the "new Elvis Presley" go over? "I'm certain most mature theatergoers will welcome the change in Presley," he wrote. "Now as to his squealing teen-age fans—it is hoped they also will go along with the metamorphosis."

Constance Littlefield reviewed the picture in the Los Angeles *Examiner* (11/17/60), pointing out that, "The surprise of 'G.I. Blues' is Elvis himself. Shorn of sideburns, he comes through as a young man of great appeal, not only for his adoring bobby soxers, but for the maternal instinct in older women. He shows a flair for comedy and acting ability in more serious moments."

*Film Daily's* Mandel Herbstman called it "a merry, tuneful romp," and found that its "all around production treatment is a competent one and it is a sound conclusion that the large following of Presley will be delighted with his latest effort."

In the Los Angeles *Times* Margaret Harford hailed the Army for having "made a sophisticate of Presley." She added hastily that Tex Harrison and George Sanders didn't "have anything to worry about. He still needs practice. But a polished Elvis is the news in 'G.I. Blues.' " She also celebrated Elvis' new haircut, "a trim job that gives him an unaccustomed look of tidiness. Gone too are the rock 'n' roll wiggle and that old lecherous leer....You can almost like him."

(14) "GIRLS, GIRLS, GIRLS" — A Paramount release. Produced by Hal Wallis. Directed by Norman Taurog. Associate producer: Paul Nathan. Screenplay: Edward Anhalt and Allan Weiss. Story: Allan Weiss. Photography: Loyal Griggs. Art direction: Hal Pereira and Walter Tyler. Set decoration: Sam Comer and Frank R. McKelvy. Music scorer-conductor: Joseph J. Lilley. Choreog-

raphy: Charles J. O'Curran. Sound: Harold Lewis and Charles Grenzbach. Film editor: Stanley E. Johnson. Assistant director: D. Michael Moore. Filmed in Technicolor. Running time: 101 minutes.

*Cast:* Elvis Presley, Stella Stevens, Jeremy Strauss, Guy Lee, Frank Puglia, Lilli Valenty, and Beulah Quo.

Elvis starred in the role of Ross Carpenter, a poor fisherman who meets a wealthy girl who falls in love with him, forgetting to tell him how rich she realy is.

*Reviews:* In *Variety* (11/7/62) *Dale.* noted that the film "hinges on the popularity of the entertainer, who is given a plethora of songs regardless of whether they fit smoothly into the action." But he did report that Elvis "handles the role capably."

Margaret Harford of The Los Angeles *Times* (11/23/62) found it to be "no better or worse than previous Elvis epics. It's just a question of whether you can take it." She also pointed out that it reunited Elvis with Hal Wallis, which "may explain why America's singing idol, noticeably subdued in recent movies, is back in his old swivel-hipped form."

James Powers in The Hollywood *Reporter* (11/2/62) said Elvis "performs with his usual style and on some numbers demonstrates a growing maturity of voice. His distinctive body movements seem to indicate, also, that he has been ahead of his time: what he was doing was only what is known today as the 'twist'."

(15) "GIRL HAPPY" — An MGM release. Produced by Joe Pasternak. Directed by Boris Segal. Screenplay: Harvey Bullock and R.S. Allen.

Photography: Philip H. Lathrop. Art direction: George W. Davis and Addison Hehr. Set decoration: Henry Grace and Hugh Hunt. Music: George Stoll. Sound: Franklin Milton. Film editor: Rita Roland. Assistant director: Jack Aldworth. Filmed in Metrocolor and Panavision. Running time: 96 mnutes.

*Cast:* Elvis Presley, Shelley Fabares, Harold J. Stone, Gary Crosby, Jody Baker, Nita Talbot, Mary Ann Mobley, Fabrizio Mioni, Jimmy Hawkins, Jackie Coogan, Peter Brooks, John Fiedler, Chris Noel, Lyn Edgington, Gale Gilmore, Pamela Curran and Rusty Allen.

Elvis played the part of Rusty Wells, a musician from a Chicago nightclub who is sent to keep an eye on the owner's daughter who is in Fort Lauderdale, Florida for the annual Easter vacation migration of college students to that beach city.

*Reviews:* In *Variety* (1/27/65) *Whit.* called the film "another musical winner" for Elvis. He found it to have "a story line unburdened by anything but lightness and a dozen song numbers belted out in the singer's customary style." All in all, "the type of pleasant fare which Presley's fans have come to expect."

James Powers wrote in The Hollywood *Reporter* (1/21/65) that the movie "should do the customary brisk Presley business." He added that, "Presley's forte is not comedy, but he has good backing in the trio of actors who play members of his combo, Gary Crosby, Jody Baker and Jimmy Hawkins."

*Motion Picture Daily's* William R. Weaver observed (1/21/65) that "With product like this going for him, Elvis Presley's status in Quigley

Publications' Money-Making Stars polling—which placed him sixth on the Top Ten list for 1964, his fourth year on the list—can't go any way but up."

Calling it "a snug fit for the Presley talents," Weaver said, "He's got the undertaking comfortably under control from start to finish and seems to enjoy it as much as his audiences will."

(16) "HARUM SCARUM" — An MGM release. Produced by Sam Katzman. Directed by Gene Nelson. Screenplay: Gerald Drayson Adams. Photography: Fred H. Jackman. Art direction: George W. Davis and H. McClure Capps. Set decoration: Henry Grace and Don Greenwood Jr. Music: Fred Karger. Sound: Franklin Milton. Film editor: Ben Lewis. Assistant director: Eddie Saeta. Filmed in Metrocolor. Running time: 95 minutes.

*Cast:* Elvis Presley, Mary Ann Mobley, Fran Jeffries, Michael Ansara, Jay Novello, Philip Reed, Theo Marcuse, Billy Barty, Dick Harvey, Jack Costanzo, Larry Chance, Barbara Werle, Brenda Benet, Gail Gilmore, Wilda Taylor, Vicki Malikin, Rick Rydon, Richard Reeves and Joey Russo.

Elvis played the role of Johnny Tyrone, a Hollywood star visiting the Mid-East for the opening of his latest big movie.

*Revies:* In *Variety* (10/27/65) *Whit.* charged that, "With anybody but Elvis Presley to gun possibilities this would be a pretty dreary affair at the box office. Elvis, however, apparently can do no wrong." He complained that "Harum Scarum" suffered "from a lack of imagination in providing the star with a substantial showcase." But did grant that thanks to the eight songs Elvis sings the film "will probably meet with response similar to Presley's past entries."

Dale Munroe reviewed the film in The Hollywood *Citizen-News* (11/27/65) and decided that "this cinematic farce just doesn't come off." He suggested that it "is likely to be enjoyed primarily by Presley's most avid fans."

In The Hollywood *Reporter* (10/22/65) James Powers noted that the movie "seems to have all the usual ingredients that make his films a success." As for Elvis, he "continues to handle himself naturally, no different in manner or appearance than in his earliest films."


(17) "IT HAPPENED AT THE WORLD'S FAIR" — An MGM release. Produced by Ted Richmond. Directed by Norman Taurog. Screenplay: Si Rose and Seaman Jacobs. Photography: Joseph Ruttenberg. Art direction: George W. Davis and Preston Ames. Set decoration: Henry Grace and Hugh Hunt. Music: Keith Stevens. Sound: Franklin Milton. Film editor: Frederic Steinkamp. Assistant director: Al Jennings. Filmed in Metrocolor and Panavision. Running time: 105 minutes.

*Cast:* Elvis Presley, Joan O'Brien, Gary Lockwood, Vicky Tiu, H.M. Wynant, Edith Atwater, Guy Raymond, Dorothy Green, Kam Tong and Yvonne Craig.

Elvis starred as Mike Edwards, a barnstorming, crop-dusting pilot who winds up in Seattle at the World's Fair, where there are plenty of girls to occupy him.

*Reviews:* The question raised by *Tube.* in his *Daily Variety* review (4/1/63) was, "whether the star's mighty popularity is surviving into the new wave of youngsters coming along to replace his former fans, who are moving out of the idolatry of adolescence and into maturity."

He complained that the 10 Presley songs in the film wound up being "interruptions (which) upset the tempo of the yarn, frivolous as it is, and prevent plot and picture from gathering momentum."

The Hollywood *Reporter's* James Powers said (4/2/63) that Elvis "handles himself well and in several songs displays what seems a new vocal style, with some of his reedier tones eliminated and a generally more melodic pattern."

In The New York *Times* Eugene Archer took a crack at the film, charging that Elvis' "budding dramatic talents have been neatly nipped in the Seattle story, which emerges as a dismal parody of the Metro-Goldwyn-Mayer musicals of old." He added that, "the crooner merely swivels ingenuously through a morass of cliches."

(18) "JAILHOUSE ROCK" — An MGM release. Produced by Pandro S. Berman. Directed by Richard Thorpe. Screenplay: Guy Trosper. Based on a story by Ned Young. Photography: Robert Bronner. Art direction: William A Horning and Randall Duell. Set decoration: Henry Grace and Keogh Gleason. Music supervisor: Jeff Alexander. Recording supervisor: Dr. Wesley C. Miller. Film editor: Ralph E. Winters. Filmed in CinemaScope. Running time: 96 minutes.

*Cast:* Elvis Presley, Judy Tyler, Mickey Shaughnessy, Vaughn Taylor, Jennifer Holden, Dean Jones and Anne Neyland.

Elvis had the role of Vince Everett, who winds up

in jail for killing a bum in a bar-room brawl.

*Reviews: Variety* reviewer *Whit.* wrote (10/16/-57) that the movie "is packed with type of sure-fire ingredients producers know Presley's followers go for, and it's likely a considerable portion of the populace...will find this Metro release in their alley." He did point out that, Elvis "is still no great shakes as an actor, but gets by well enough."

James Powers noted in The Hollywood *Reporter* (10/16/57) that MGM had faced the problem of "broadening the appeal (of Elvis) without losing the royal segment you started with." He said the "result is not a 'new' Elvis, but the old Presley seems toned down to the extent that his distinctive mannerisms are less florid."

(19) "KID GALAHAD" — A United Artists release. Produced by David Weisbart. Directed by Phil Karlson. Screenplay: William Fay. Based on a story by Francis Wallace. Photography: Burnett Guffey. Art direction: Cary Odell. Set decoration: Edward G. Boyle. Music: Jeff Alexander. Sound: Lambert Day. Film editor: Stuart Gilmore. Assistant director: Jerome M. Siegel. Filmed in color by DeLuxe. Running time: 94 minutes.

*Cast:* Elvis Presley, Gig Young, Lola Albright, Joan Blackman, Charles Bronson, Ned Glass, Robert Emhardt, David Lewis, Michael Dante, Judson Pratt, George Mitchell, Richard Devon, Jeffrey Morris and Liam Redmond.

Elvis was cast in the role of Walter Gulick, a handsome ex-soldier who becomes a boxer almost by accident.

*Reviews: Daily Variety* (7/25/62) noted that

Elvis' "vast following doesn't seem to have diminished appreciably over the years in spite of the subtle alteration of his public image from the swivel-hipped, side-burn adorned hound dog howler into the mellowed, mannerly matinee idol that he is today."

The paper added that, "Presley's acting resources are limited, but he has gradually established a character with which he doesn't have to strain too much for emtional nuance—the soft-spoken, unaffected, polite, unspoiled, forthright and ultimately two-fisted country boy." Note was also made of Elvis having put on some weight in this picture, which "is not especially becoming."

The Hollywood *Reporter* (7/25/62) thought it was "a good vehicle for the talents of Elvis Presley," and said that the star "is likeable and convincing as the bashful, gallant boxer."

Bosley Crowther, writing in The New York *Times* (3/7/63), observed that, "Mr. Presley does not make a very convincing pug." But he felt that the film was "a moderately genial entertainment. It's not explosive, but it has the cheerful top of a lightly romantic contrivance that ranges between comedy and spoof. For this we can thank the other actors."

(20) "KING CREOLE" — A Paramount release. Produced by Hal B. Wallis. Directed by Michael Curtiz. Screenplay: Michael V. Gazzo and Herbert Baker. Based on the novel "A Stone for Danny Fisher" by Harold Robbins. Photography: Russell Harland. Music: arranged and conducted by Walter Scharf. Choreography: Charles O'Curran. Film editor: Warren Low. Filmed in black-and-white. Running time: 116 minutes.

*Cast:* Elvis Presley, Carolyn Jones, Walter Matthau, Dolores Hart, Dean Jagger, Lillane Montevecchi, Vic Morrow, Paul Stewart, Jan Sheapard, Brian Hutton, Jack Grinnage, Dick Winslow and Raymond Bailey.

Elvis had the role of Danny Fisher, as a troubled high school student with a lot of muscial talent.

*Reviews: Variety's Powe.* thought (5/28/58) that the film "shows the young star this time as a better-than-fair actor." He said it might not win Elvis any new fans, "but it won't, at any rate, provoke new attacks" on him.

In the Beverly Hills *Citizen* (7/9/58) Hazel Flynn wrote that in "King Creole" Elvis "does his best actмng. I predicted from the first that Elvis might make a fair actor someday and I still think so. After he gets out of the Army and is a little more serious in his viewpoint on life, his virility and natural dramatic ability should be welcome in serious roles and he shouldn't have to rock that geetar at all."

S.A. Desick of the Los Angeles *Examiner* commented (7/4/58) that, "The youthful votaries who dig Elvis Presley can shriek their homage anew to the rock-and-roll deity." He continued, "With such a profusion of music, I wonder whether Elvis' partisans will notice that he has improved somewhat as an actor....Elvis' role requires a certain sensitivity. Surprisingly, he displays flashes of this if only intermittently."

In the Los Angeles *Mirror-News* (8/4/58) Margaret Hartford wrote that " 'King Creole' is probably the strongest of Presley's...film ventures." She noted that he, "is no longer depicted as the churlish, egotistical singing idol."

**233**

(21) "KISSIN' COUSINS — An MGM release. Produced by Sam Katzman. Directed by Gene Nelson. Screenplay: Gerald Drayson Adams and Gene Nelson. Story: Gerald Drayson Adams. Photography: Ellis W. Carter. Art direction: George W. Davis and Eddie Imazu. Set decoration: Henry Grace and Budd S. Friend. Music: Fred Karger. Sound: Franklin Milton. Film editor: Ben Lewis. Assistant director: Eli Dunn. Filmed in Metrocolor and Panavision. Running time: 96 minutes.

*Cast:* Elvis Presley, Arthur O'Connell, Glenda Farrell, Jack Albertson, Pam Austin, Cynthia Pepper, Yvonne Craig, Donald Woods, Tommy Farrell, Beverly Powers, Hortense Petra and Robert Stone.

Elvis played the twin roles of Josh Morgan and Jodie Tatum, one an Air Force lieutenant trying to establish a missile base on some land owned by hillbillies, the other his country cousin who just happens to look exactly like him (except for having blonde hair).

*Reviews: Variety's Tube.* took a dim view of "Kissin' Cousins," writing 3/4/64 that "this new Elvis Presley concoction is a pretty dreary effort." The point made was that Elvis "needs—and merits—more susbstantial material than this if his career is to flourish as in the past."

Another complaint was that, "smoother, slicker, more convincing techniques for lapsing into song are necessary in the modern musical." As for Elvis, "Histrionically, Presley does as well as possible under the circumstances."

On the other hand, The Hollywood *Reporter's* James Powers thought (3/5/64) that the picture "gives the reliable singing star a fine showcase in an amusing double role." He predicted that "the hillbilly musical comedy should be one of Presley's strongest hits. All Presley's pictures do well, but this one should be outstanding." In terms of Elvis' own work, "Presley does nicely in his two roles and handles himself gracefully in the dance routines," was Powers' comment.

George H. Jackson, critic for the Los Angeles *Herald-Examiner,* commented (3/19/64) that, "Hollywood comes up with an answer to The Beatles by offering two, yes two, Elvis Presleys in his newest film." He called it "a gay romp, sure to please Elvis' fans," although noting that "acting demands upon the singing personality are kept to a minimum."

(22) "LIVE A LITTLE, LOVE A LITTLE" — An MGM release. Produced by Douglas Laurence. Directed by Norman Raurog. Screenplay: Michael A. Hoey and Dan Greenberg. Based on the novel, "Kiss My Firm But Pliant Lips" by Dan Greenberg. Photography: Fred Konekamp. Art direction: Geroge W. Davis and Preston Ames. Set decoration: Henry Grace and Don Greenwood Jr. Music: Billy Strange. Sound: Franklin Milton. Film editor: John McSweeney. Assistant director: Al Shenberg. Filmed in Technicolor and Panavision. Running time: 89 minutes.

*Cast:* Elvis Presley, Michele Carey, Don Porter, Rudy Vallee, Dick Sargent, Sterling Holloway, Celeste Yarnall, Eddie Hodges, Joan Shawlee,

Mary Grover, Emily Banks, Michael Keller, Merri Ashley, Phyliss Davis and Thordis Brandt.

Elvis played the role of Greg, a high fashion photographer on the one hand, and a girlie magazine photographer on the other.

*Reviews: Murf.* wrote in *Variety* (10/9/68) that this was "one of his dimmest vehicles...Songs are full, physical values are standard, and mediocrity prevails."

John Mahoney said in the Hollywood *Reporter* that "Musically anemic as well, the film has been stretched with protracting entrances and exits to just under an hour and a half for comfy slotting in double berths."

Louis Pelegrine reviewed it in *Film-TV Daily* (10/18/68), pointing out that, "The production may not be a whizbang as movies go, but what matters as far as the box office is concerned is that it contains all the tried-and-true ingredients that go into the concoction of a standard Presley opus-romance, song, gayety, a bit of spice, frothiness, a fair number of laughs, a simple story." He concluded that, "the picture is a bright little comedy which those who are too fussy will find reasonably entertaining."

In *Motion Picture Herald* (10/2/68) Lincoln Kaye gave the picture a "fair" rating. He noted that "audiences may be excused for growing a little weary of psychological studies of frigidity."


(23) "LOVE ME TENDER" — A Twentieth Century-Fox release. Produced by David Weisbart. Directed by Robert Webb. Screenplay: Robert Buckner. Based on a story by Maurice Geraghty. Songs: Elvis Presley and Vera Matson. Photo-

graphy: Leo Tover. Running time: 94 minutes. Filmed in black-and-white and CinemaScope.

*Cast:* Richard Egan Debra Paget, Elvis Presley, Robert Middleton, William Campbell, Neville Brand, Mildred Dunnock, Bruce Bennett, James Drury, Russ Conway, Ken Clark, Barry Coe, L.Q. Jones, Paul Burns and Jerry Sheldon.

Elvis played the role of Clint, one of four brothers who, because he was the youngest, stayed home on their farm in Texas while the others were off fighting in the Civil War.

*Reviews:* This was Elvis' first motion picture appearance, and it received a great deal of attention in the press. Writing in *Variety* (11/21/56) *Gros.* explained that Fox "has whipped up a minor league oater...in which to showcase one of the hottest show biz properties around today. It's a box office natural for the screaming set and some elders may even wander in and out of curiosity." He also noted that, "Appraising Presley as an actor, he ain't. Not that it makes much difference. The presence of Presely apparently is enough to satisfy the juve set."

Unlike most of the Elvis pictures to follow, "Love Me Tender" contained only four songs. As *Gros.* reported, "the title tune already a 100,000,000 plus disk seller.'

Hollis Alpert, in the *Saturday Review* (12/8/56), commented that, "The incomprehensible Presley is a triple-threat man in this one: he sings, he wiggles, and he acts."

*Time* (11/26/56) said that Elvis "all but steals the show from such better-known players as Richard Egan, Debra Paget and Mildred Dunnock. Hollywood, moreover, foresees a boxoffice bonanza when the millions who buy Presley's pressings...go to see his first picture..."

*The New Yorker's* critic (11/24/56) wrote, "Thick-lipped, droopy-eyed and indefatigably sullen, Mr. Presley, whose talents are meagre but whose earnings are gross, excites a big section of the young female population as nobody else as ever done." After seeing the picture at the old Paramount Theatre in New York's Times Square, he reported that, "the audience began to chant, "We want Elvis!" This went on for some time, until at last, Elvis Presley ambled onto the screen."

In the Los Angeles *Examiner* (11/22/56) Ruth Waterbury told her readers, "Elvis can act. S'help me, the boy's real good, even when he isn't singing, even when he is emoting, though when he gets in any very deep emotions they've turned his back to the camera." She ended by suggesting that, "Tender is not the word for 'Love Me Tender,' but 'tremendous' definitely is."

Hazel Flynn wrote in the Beverly Hills *Citizen* )11/23/56) that the film's "story is no great shakes" and its "direction uninspired." Calling it a "corny hill-billy vehicle" she confessed that, "Young Presley does a pretty good job and proves that today's kids are not so dumb. They know unusual talent when they see it."

She went on to say, "I agree that some of his movements are slightly embarrassing, but no more so that most of the jazz, jive, rock 'n roll, peckin' and other acrobatic dancing which has become popular in the last quarter of a century.

"Oddly, I don't think any of this is necessary to Elvis any longer. It garnered him attention and publicity. Now he can taper off and go over to straight acting, saving his folk singing and stomping for personal appearances."

She concluded by writing, "Shame on you, 20th Century-Fox for not giving our Elvis a better deal. After all, there's something besides money...or is there?"

Dick Williams wrote in the Los Angeles *Mirror-News* (11/22/56) that, "Without Elvis, the film would be just an average, cheaply made western action movie with a lot of hard riding and shooting, chases, stickups and the rest of the old bag of shopworn tricks. But with him it may be a box-office bonanza." He noted that Elvis "does a reasonably good job for his first time out on the acting assignment."

He also indicated that Robert Wagner or Jeff Hunter might have had the role Elvis got in the original plan to make the picture as "The Reno Brothers." But Fox's production chief, Buddy Adler, had pushed for Elvis in the role and had gotten him.

As for the reaction in Los Angeles theatres when the picture was shown, Williams reported, "Elvis does not appear on screen until about 10 minutes of the picture...has unfolded. When he does...the teenage girls began to squeal at the showing I attended. It's an eerie sensation to hear this mass hysteria and one which tends to raise the hair on your neck."

In his Los Angeles *Times* column (11/4/56) Philip K. Scheuer wrote about "Love Me Tender." He quoted the film's producer, David Weisbart, at length in a fascinating interview.

"I think he (Elvis) provides a tremendous additional value in the role," Weisbart stated. "He will surprise a lot of people who go to see him because his presence is just a gimmick. Actually he plays an acting part in a legitmate story and does it very well. He sings, but the script is so constructed that the situations are logical."

How was Elvis to work with? "Here at the studio we found him humble, polite, solicitous, nothing like his reputation—'lewed,' 'corrupting' and so on. In fact, he's a lot like all of us would like to be—easy, with a certain kind of independence. But perhaps nobody except young people can understand him fully: he is the equivalent of being cool."

Asked to contrast Elvis and James Dean, Weisbart is quoted as having replied: "Elvis is extroverted, gregarious on a young person's level, terribly energetic, seems to be having fun. He was cooperative with us, never late and very serious about acting. This was another kind of career for him, a big challenge after all those one-night stands with screaming teenagers following him around.

"I don't think Elvis is in the same class with Dean as an actor. His biggest asset is his own natural quality, like Gary Cooper's. If he acquires any of the obvious acting skills, they might hurt him.

"Jimmy, on the other hand, was introverted, more complicated. He achieved in his acting the thing Elvis had without acting—which made Jimmy the better actor in the acting sense—if you follow me."

He added, "Youngsters felt more of a brooding identification with Dean in his role of the misunderstood teenager—a universal complaint of kids!"

They worked in different media, too. "You must remember, though, that Dean was seen only on film. Elvis plays to an audience, he exciting them and they exciting him. Hero worship enters here: this is a guy who picked up a guitar somewhere and became a millionaire! Every kid with a harmonica dreams of doing the same thing.

"I believe it is good in a way for kids to go to the theater and watch their idols, if only as a release for their excess energies. Their chances of getting into trouble, I'd say, are diminished rather than increased."

How did the picture do? It was a box office smash, of course! The Hollywood *Reporter* ran a front page lead story about it under the headline, "PRESLEY PIC NEGATIVE COST BEING COVERED WITHIN THE FIRST MONTH OF NATIONAL RELEASE." That paper said that the film "is on the way to paying off its negative cost in two weeks after its national release—the first instance of its kind for a major production." "Love Me Tender" cost not very much over $1,000,000 to produce. In the *Variety* anniversary edition of January, 1976 in the list of "All-Time Film Rental Champs," it was reported that the total film rentals for "Love Me Tender" are estimated at $4,200,000. Rentals are the portion of box office gross that the film distributor receives. So Fox, apparently, made something on the order of over $3 million profit on its "introduction" of Elvis to movie audiences. Not bad at all, considering that movie tickets cost a lot less in 1956 than they do today.

(24) "LOVING YOU" — A Paramount release. Produced by Hal Wallis. Directed by Hal Kanter. Associate producer: Paul Nathan. Screenplay: Herbert Baker and Hal Kanter. From a story by Mary Agnes Thompson. Photography: Charles Lang. Color consultant: Richard Mueller. Art direction: Hal Pereira and Albert Nozaki. Set decoration: Sam Comer and Ray Moyer. Music arranger/conductor: Walter Scharf. Numbers staged by Charles O'Curran. Vocal accompaniment: The Jordanaires. Sound: Hugo and Charles Grenzbach. Film editor: Howard Smith. Filmed in Technicolor and Vista-Vision. Running time: 102 minutes.

*Cast:* Elvis Presley, Lizabeth Scott, Wendell Corey, James Gleason, Ralph Dumke, Paul Smith, Ken Becker, Jana Lund, Dolores Hart and Gail Land.

Elvis had the starring role of Deke Rivers, a young guitarist who becomes a hit when he joins a small hillbilly band.

*Reviews:* In *Variety* 7/3/57) *Hift.* observed, "Though the rock 'n' roll craze perhaps passed its peak, there's little question that a sizeable part of the citizenry will welcome Elvis Presley back for his second screen appearance."

The picture, he wrote, is "a simple story, in which he can be believed, which has romantic overtones and exposes the singer to the kind of thing he does best." He also pointed to the fact that Elvis "shows improvement as an actor. It's not a demanding part and, being surrounded by a capable crew of performers, he comes across as a simple but pleasant sort."

James Powers wrote in The Hollywood *Reporter* (7/3/57) that the problem with Elvis' new movie is that "young girls, and some not so young, set up ear-splitting screams almost every time Presley appeared on screen." He added tht Elvis "acts naturally and with appeal. He would be attractive to a member of the older generation if the picture could be seen without the maddening female chorus."

Edwin Schallert wrote in the Los Angeles *Times* (7/31/57) that "Presley may still be able to win with crowds in person and possibly on television, but the film is as yet a vast uncharted sea for him...An entirely new personality will have to be discovered for him on the screen just as it was finally for Frank Sinatra, who had a much brighter and more persistent start."

He found less screaming in the theatres than Powers had heard. "I had the impression that the reception accorded the wonder boy of the rock 'n' roll was scarcely even mild, where it has been frantic and wild on past occasions." Still, he thought the new film "can probably be reckoned a furtive step forward on Presley's part in a screen career."

In the Los Angeles *Examiner* (8/1/57) Ruth Waterbury called the movie "the utter end, the living most, not alone if you belong to the passionate legions of Presley worshippers but also if sharp, tremendous personalities interest you." She said, that "as one who grew up in the era when Rudy Vallee...was considered 'wicked,' I can take the 'wickedness' Presley represents to some older people with equanimity." She summed up that, "for teenagers this will be a thrill, for their elders an experience, and for all concerned, fun."

(25) "PARADISE, HAWAIIAN STYLE" — A Parmount release. Produced by Hal Wallis. Directed by Michael Moore. Associate Producer: Paul Nathan. Screenplay: Allan Weiss and Anthony Lawrence. Story: Allan Weiss. Photography: W. Wallace Kelley. Art direction: Hal Pereira and Walter Tyler. Set decoration: Sam Comer and Ray Moyer. Music: Joseph J. Lilley. Sound: John Carter: Film editor: Warren Low. Assistant director: James Rosenberg. Assistant to the producer: Jack Saper. Filmed in Technicolor. Running time: 90 minutes.

*Cast:* Elvis Presley, Suzanna Leigh, James Shigeta, Donna Butterworth, Marianna Hill, Irene Tsu, Linda Wong, Julie Parrish, Jan Shepard, John Doucette, Philip Ahn, Grady Sutton, Dan Collier, Doris Packer, Mary Treen and Gi Gi Verone.

Elvis played the role of Rich Richards, an adventurous young pilot with a taste for pretty girls.

*Reviews: Daily Variety* (6/6/66) considered this the "type of yarn he's best suited for...girls and songs." The paper noted that, "Presley delivers one of his customary ingratiating portrayals in usual voice and adept at comedy.

Mandel Herbstman wrote in *Film Daily* (6/8/66) that the picture "has the stamp of popular appeal all over it." He cited it as having followed "the successful formula of past Presley hits."

In the Hollywood *Reporter* (6/6/66) James Powers said, "It is not one of the best Presley films in incident and development, but it should satisfy the fans, and has some good Hawaiian dance numbers to beef it up." He added that, "Presley seems to have developed a new vocal style in some of his songs, a fuller, more robust voice. It sounds good."

Los Angeles *Times'* critic Kevin Thomas called it "pleasant hot weather diversion. Pretty much the usual Elvis Presley formula of songs and romance." As for Elvis, "as always (he) remains relaxed, enjoyable entertainer."


(26) "ROUSTABOUT" — A Parmount release. Produced by Hall Wallis. Directed by John Rich. Associate Producer: Paul Nathan. Screenplay: Anthony Lawrence and Allan Weiss. Story: Allan Weiss. Photography: Lucien Ballard. Art direction: Sam Comer and Robert Benton. Music: Joseph J. Lilley. Sound: John Carter and Charles Grenzbach. Film editor: Warren Low. Assistant director: D. Michael Moore. Filmed in Technicolor and Techniscope. Running time: 101 minutes.

*Cast:* Elvis Presley, Barbara Stanwyck, Joan Freeman, Leif Erikson, Sue Ann Langdon, Pat Buttram, Joan Staley, Dabs Greer, Steve Brodie, Norman Grabowski, Jack Albertson, Jane Dulo, Joel Fluellen and Wilda Taylor.

Elvis played the role of Charlie Rogers, a young vagabond singer who joins a carnival.

*Reviews: Variety's Hogg.* (11/11/64) found this to be "a gaudily-staged, tritely-scripted film looming as a box office smash based on lure of Presley name." He noted that, "good cast tries it best to cope with nonsense but it's a losing battle."

In the Hollywood *Reporter* (11/11/64) James Powers hailed it as "one of the best pictures Elvis Presley has made and should be one of the best box office draws." He also said that its "threadbare theme has been rewoven with skill, the trimmings are fancy, and 'Roustabout' should be a rousing success."

As for Elvis, he "creates a likeable and believable character. he is at his best, to be sure, in the musical department."

John G. Houser of the Los Angeles *Herald-Examiner* (11/27/64) called it "a rousing, thrilling story coupled with some outstanding tunes...the best Elvis Presley movie of his cinema career."

He said it was "jam-packed with action, romance, colorful characters and musical numbers that complement each other and add up to a mammoth entertainment package." Notable also is that, "Elvis' proficiency at karate is demonstrated several times." He concluded that in the film "Elvis has everything going for him and he uses it all to best advantage. It's his best and worth seeing."

The Hollywood *Citizen News'* (11/26/64) critic Nadine M. Edwards pointed to "Roustabout" as "another of those lightly-paced dramatic musicals which seem to be Elvis' forte. He doesn't have to do much but he always manages to please his many followers with his easy going manner of acting and his (admittedly) sexy way of presenting a song."

(27) "SPEEDWAY" — An MGM release. Produced by Douglas Laurance. Directed by Norman Taurog. Screenplay: Phillip Shuken. Photography: Joseph Ruttenberg. Art direction: Geroge Davis and LeRoy Coleman. Set decoration: Henry Grace and Don Greenwood, Jr. Music: Jeff Alexander. Sound: Franklin Milton. Film editor: Richard Farrell. Assistant director: Dale Hutchin-

son. Fimed in Metrocolor and Panavision. Running time: 92 minutes.

*Cast:* Elvis Presley, Nancy Sinatra, Bill Bixby, Gale Gordon, William Schalert, victoria Meyer-nick, Ross Hagen, Carl Ballentine, Poncie Ponce, Harry Kickos and Christopher West.

Elvis played the role of Steve Grayson, an auto racer who finds himself owing the IRS $145,000.

*Reviews: Whit.* wrote in *Variety* (5/17/68) that, "an Elvis Presley film is money in the bank, regardless of story or who appears with him." He felt that "the story lacks the legitimacy of the better Presley starrers," but that it should do well with audiences anyway. "Aside from Presley's singing, however, most of the interest rests in exciting stock car racing footage, lensed at the Charlotte Speedway in North Carolina," he told readers.

Ray Loynd of The Hollywood *Reporter* (5/17/68) criticized the film for having a plot that is "tissue-thin and souped up with a cloying sub-plot involving Presley's charity to a poverty-stricken father." But he agreed that "it's bound to make money by merely adhering to the regular distribution pattern."

Kevin Thomas was even more critical in the Los Angeles *Times* (8/8/68), saying that it "has a script that ran out of gas before Elvis Presley was born." He stated that, "Presley pictures can be unpretentious fun, but this one is both uninspired and too much of an imitation of too many of his previous movies."

(28) "SPINOUT". — An MGM release. Produced by Joe Pasternak. Directed by Norman

Taurog. Associate producer: Hank Moonjean. Screenplay: Theodore J. Flicker and George Kirgo. Art direction: George W. Davis and Edward Carfagno. Set decoration: Henry Grace and Hugh Hunt. Music: George Stoll. Sound: Franklin Milton. Film editor: Rita Roland. Assistant director: Claude Binyon Jr. Filmed in Metrocolor and Panavision. Running time: 93 minutes.

*Cast:* Elvis Presley, Shelley Fabares, Diane McBain, Deborah Walley, Dodie Marshall, Jack Mullaney, Will Hutchins, Warren Berlinger, Jimmy Hawkins, Carl Betz, Cecil Kellaway, Una Merkel, Frederic Worlock and Dave Barry.

Elvis played the role of Mike McCoy a top race driver who also happens to be an excellent singer.

*Reviews:* In *Variety* (10/19/66) *Murf.* cited the film as "an entertaining Elvis Presley comedy tuner." He noted that it was part of the "current Parker-Presley film formula of three per year—Easter, summer and now." The "now" was pre-Thanksgiving. Those are the three times of the year during which the movie business does it very best. So the scheduling of Elvis' releases was nothing short of inspired.

The Hollywood *Reporter's* James Powers wrote that, " 'Spinout' is a bright collection of fair humor and good musical numbers. That looks like it should be the RX for Presley fans and younger audiences generally."

*Time,* which never seemed to like Presley films, complained that "eleven years of living high on the hawg...has emphatically porked up his appearance. His cheeks are now so plump that he looks like a kid blowing bubble gum—and his mouth is still so squiggly that it looks as if the bubble had burst. What's more, he now sports a glossy something on his summit that adds at least five inches to his altitude, and looks like a swatch of hot buttered yak wool."

As a final insult, *Time* (11/11/66) said, "For Presley, immobility may signify maturity. He is pitching his act at some sort of adult audience— possibly adult chimpanzees."

Kevin Thomas wrote in the Los Angeles *Times* that, "There's no doubt about it: both Elvis Presley and his pictures get better all the time. 'Tickle Me' had plenty of pizazz, and "Frankie and Johnny' was a fine little film—but the first was spoiled by a lousy script and color and the second cried for stronger production values. Now comes 'Spinout,' perhaps his best picture yet—with none of the past detriments and some new pluses."

The opposite point of view was espoused by Nadine M. Edwards in the Hollywood *Citizen-News* (8/9/68). "Elvis has what is probably his weakest role to date, a surprising departure for the singer who has chalked up such a fine box office record through the years," she wrote.

Her criticism focused on the picture screenplay which "is one of the most inept and inconsequential, albeit inocuous, pieces of nothing upon which any writer ever labored."

(29) "STAY AWAY JOE!" — An MGM release. Produced by Douglas Laurence. Directed by Peter Tewksbury. Screenplay: Michael A. Hoey. Based on the novel by Dan Cushman. Photography: Fred Konekamp. Art direction: George W. Davis and

Carl Anderson. Set decoration: Henry Grace and Don Greenwood Jr. Music: Jack Marshall. Sound: Franklin Milton. Film editor: George W. Brooks. Assistant director: Dale Hutchinson. Filmed in Metrocolor and Panavision. Running time: 101 minutes.

*Cast:* Elvis Presley, Burgess Meredith, Joan Blondell, Katy Jurado, Thomas Gomez, Henry Jones, L.Q. Jones, Quentin Dean, Anne Seymour, Douglas Henderson, Angus Duncan, Michael Lane, Susan Trustman, Warren Vanders, Buck Kartalian, Maurishka, Caitlan Wyles, Marya Christen, Sonny West, Jennifer Peak, Brett Parker and Michael Keller.

Elvis played the role of Joe Lightcloud, a vagabond rodeo champ.

*Reviews: Variety* (3/8/68) found it to be a "generally flat comedy." *Murf.* said that, "at best, film is a dim artistic accomplishment; at worst, it caters to out-dated prejudice." He also noted that, "thin  plot line is threaded with many forced slapstick situations, in which the players seem to be having a ball, although the enthusiasm rarely transmits from screen to audience."

Mandel Herbstman wrote in *Film Daily* (3/11/68) that, "the film has all the formulas and familiar Presley touches that assure it popularity in given markets." He went on to say that, "it doesn't matter that credibility is stretched. What matters is that the picture evokes a mood of mirth and happy frenzy that is catching."

John Mahoney didn't care for the picture much either. He declared in the Hollywood *Reporter* (3/8/68) that, "the film moves with the boisterous vulgarity of a marathon beer bust, though its quaint and patronizing view of American Indians as brawling, balling, boozing children should rightly offend many or all."

In the Hollywood *Citizen-News* (4/27/68) Arnold Rabbin observed that, "When a talent of the quality of Elvis Presley comes on the scene, when that talent is greeted with superlatives from the very outset, and when that person manages to sustain those superlatives—blemish free—for nearly 15 years, we can only assume that he must be doing something right." To him this picture "marks just another brilliantly executed step in the making of another Bing Crosby-like career."

(30) "TICKLE ME" — An Allied Artists release. Produced by Ben Schwalb. Directed by Norman Taurog. Screenplay: Elwood Ullman and Edward Bernds. Photography: Loyal Griggs. Music: Walter Scharf. Art direction: Hal Pereira and Arthur Lonergan. Assistant director: Arthur Jacobson. Sound: Hugo Grenzbach and Charles Grenzbach. Film editor: Archie Marshek. Filmed in Color by DeLuxe. Running time: 90 minutes.

*Cast:* Elvis Presley, Julie Adams, Jocelyn Lane, Jack Mullaney, Merry Anders, Bill Williams, Edward Faulkner, Connie Gilchrist, Barbara Werle, John Dennis, Grady Sutton, Allison Hayes, Inez Pedroza, Lilyan Chauvin, Angela Greene, Louie Elias, Robert Hoy, Dorothy Konrad, Eve Bruce and Francine York.

Elvis played the role of Lonnie Beale, a rodeo rider who signs on temporarily at an Arizona dude ranch/beauty spa.

*Reviews:* In *Variety* (6/16/65) *Whit.* pointed out that, "the substantial hold that Elvis Presley wields over his public will continue." He thought Elvis got "good comedy backing from a competent cast," and noted that, "Presley takes his character in stride, giving a performance calculated to appeal particularly to his following."

*Box Office* (6/21/65) called it a film with "many moments of fun," and commented that, "While the story would hardly win an Oscar for originality, the great popularity of Presley will surmount that, as witness his strident success over the years."

Kevin Thomas of the Los Angeles *Times* (7/16/65) liked it in spite of "lousy color, cheap sets, hunks of stock footage, painted scenery and unconvincing process work." He raised the question, "Who's to quibble when the movie is so much fun?"

Thomas found Elvis to be "in great form...Besides his good voice (better than ever), his best asset is naturalness that demolishes all attempts to endow him with mythical powers."

(31) "THE TROUBLE WITH GIRLS" — An MGM release. Produced by Lester Welch. Directed by Peter Tewksbury. Screenplay: Arnold and Lois Peyser. From the novel by Day Keene and Dwight Babcock. Story: Mauri Grashin. Photography: Jacques Marquette. Art direction: George W. Davis and Edward Carfagno. Music: Billy Strange: Sound: Franklin Milton. Film editor: George W. Brooks. Set decoration: Henry Grace and Jack Mills. Choreography: Jonathan Lucas. Assistant director: John Clark Bowman. Filmed in Metro-

color and Panavision. Running time: 97 minutes. MPAA rating: G/general audiences.

*Cast:* Elvis Presley, Marilyn Mason, Nicole Jaffe, Sheree North, Edward Andrews, John Carradine, Anissa Jones, Vincent Price, Joyce Van Patten, Pepe Brown, Dabney Coleman, Bill Zuckert, Pitt Herbert, Anthony Teague, Med Flory, Robert Nichols, Helene Winston, Kevin O'Neal, Frank Welker, John Rubinstein, Chuck Briles, Patsy Garrett, Linda Sue Risk, Charles P. Thompson, Leonard Rumery, William M. Paris, Kathleen Rainey, Hal James Pederson, Mike Wagner, Brett Parker, Duke Snider and the Pacific Palisades High School Madrigals.

Elvis played the part of Walter Hale, the manager of a 1920's Chautaugua theatre circuit attraction called "The Rolling Canvas College."

*Reviews: Variety's Whit.* (5/15/69) thought Elvis was "lost in this one." With Elvis' songs "cut down to a bare three, picture has little to offer."

He noted that, "title suggests a gay comedy but it's a mass of contrived melodramatics and uninteresting performances that do not jell into anything but program fare."

*Film-Television Daily's* Louis Pelegrin called it "a lackluster affair." He wrote that, "the film is one that does not require much in the way of acting from its cast. The players are content to walk through their roles."

William Tusher of The Hollywood *Reporter* (5/14/69) wrote that, "should Presley loyalists be willing to settle for no more than the assurance that their idol is alive and living in Hollywood, the picture will be graced by purpose." He did find a more mature Elvis, however—"He now smokes cigars, and he talks more grown up, too."

(32) "VIVA LAS VEGAS" — An MGM release. Produced by Jack Cummings. Directed by George Sidney. Screenplay: Sally Benson. Photography: Joseph Biroc. Art direction: George W. Davis and Edward Carfagno. Set decoration: Henry Grace and George R. Nelson. Music: George Stoll. Sound: Franklin Milton. Film editor: John McSweeney Jr. Assistant director: Milton Feldman. Filmed in Metrocolor and Panavision. Running time: 85 minutes.

*Cast:* Elvis Presley, Ann-Margaret, Cesare Danova, William Demarest and Nicky Blair.

Elvis was cast in the role of Lucky Jackson, a race car driver who wants to take part in a Grand Prix in Las Vegas.

*Reviews:* In *Variety Tube.* wrote (5/18/64) that the presence of Elvis and Ann-Margaret would "be enough to carry" the picture. But he called it "a pretty trite and heavy-handed affair, puny in story development and distortedly preoccupied with anatomical oomph."

Noting that the picture "is designed to dazzle the eyes, assault the ear and ignore the brain," he pointed out that, "any excuse to stare at a derierre in motion seems good enough for director Geroge Sidney and cameraman Joseph Biroc...but there is a certain lack of tastefulness or subtlety about the film's obsession with peeping at anatomical contours and epidermis simply for the sake of peeping."

James Powers of The Hollywood *Reporter*

observed (5/18/64) that "MGM has what will be one of Elvis Presley's biggest grossing pictures." he said, "There is a lot going on. The people are pleasant and pretty, and what is going on is lively and gay.

In the Los Angeles *Herald-Examiner* John G. Houser told readers, "the film has all the excitement and color of a Roman candle." He called Elvis and A-M "an explosive pair of dynamite performers." In his view, "Elivs is a cinch to please the femme fans and any male who doesn't like Ann-Margret is a candidate for Siberia."

Margaret Harford in the Los Angeles *Times* (7/3/64) explained that while Elvis' car has motor problems in the picture, "Nothing is wrong with the motor in our boy. It's revved up as usual. He swings, rattles and shakes through several rock-and-roll numbers. The Presley fan club, a large membership of American females from 16 to 65, will love him."

(33) "WILD IN THE COUNTRY" — A Twentieth Century-Fox release. Produced by Jerry Wald. Directed by Philip Dunne. Screenplay: Clifford Odets. Based on a novel by J.R. Salamanca. Song, "Wild in the Country," by Hugo Peretti, Luigi Creatore and George Weiss. Music: Kenyon Hopkins. Associate producer: Peter Nelson. Photography: William C. Mellor. Art direction: Jack Martin Smith and Preston Ames. Set decorations: Walter M. Scott and Stuart A. Reiss. Assistant director: Joseph E. Richards. Film editor: Dorothy Spencer. Sound: Alfred Bruzlin and Warren B. Delaplain. Filmed in Color by DeLuxe and CinemaScope. Running time: 122 minutes.

*Cast:* Elvis Presley, Hope Lange, Tuesday Weld, Millie Perkins, Rafer Johnson, John Ireland, Gary Lockwood, William Mims, Raymond Greenleaf, Christiana Crawford, Robin Raymond, Doreen Lang, Charles Arnt, Ruby Goodwin, Will Corry, Alan Napier, Jason Robards, Sr., Harry Carter, Harry Shannon and Bobby West.

Elvis played the role of Glenn, a rebellious youth mixed up with three very different girls.

*Reviews:* In *Daily Variety* (6/9/61) *Tube.* pointed out that, "Dramatically, there isn't a great deal of substance, novelty or spring to this somewhat wobbly and artificial tale." But he did think that the picture "should be acceptable as a slickly-produced, glamorously-cast hunk of romantic fiction that won't trouble the mind when one leaves the theatre."

James Powers in The Hollywood *Reporter* (6/9/61) compared the film to another famous Fox picture, calling it "a Southern 'Peyton Place.' " He felt that the picture "is contrived in its assembly, and the contrivances show."

The New York *Times'* film critic, Bosley Crowther, wrote (6/18/61) that, "even with Mr. Presley in the cast it should have been, at least, an honest drama, if not a particularly brilliant one. But it isn't. It is shamelessly dishonest. Indeed, it is downright gross in its studious distortion of human values and social realities."

He voiced his concern that American film producers were turning out pictures like this one where, "Characters are cut to fit the patterns of more and more artificial stereotypes and stories are shaped to the gross contours of suggestive, but synthetic, sex."